MAKEUPRENEUR

MAKEUPRENEUR

HOW TO BE A REAL SELF-STARTER

MARISSA DONATO

NEW DEGREE PRESS
COPYRIGHT © 2020 MARISSA DONATO
All rights reserved.

MAKEUPRENEUR
How To Be A Real Self-Starter

ISBN   978-1-64137-396-8   *Paperback*
       978-1-64137-397-5   *Kindle Ebook*
       978-1-64137-398-2   *Digital Ebook*

CONTENTS

___

ACKNOWLEDGEMENTS		7
INTRODUCTION		9
READ THIS BOOK LIKE A MAKEUPRENEUR		15
CHAPTER 1.	HUDA KATTAN—HUDA BEAUTY	19
CHAPTER 2.	HAYLEY ASHBY—BEAUTY AND THE BLING STUDIO	33
CHAPTER 3.	TAWNY GARRICK—DELUXIA BEAUTY	43
CHAPTER 4.	ASHLEY OPORTO—KISSMENOW PRODUCTS	47
CHAPTER 5.	LAVONNDRA "ELLE" JOHNSON—ELLE JOHNSON CO.	51
CHAPTER 6.	ANJALI WRENN—THE BEAUTY SUITE	55
CHAPTER 7.	ELIN DANNERSTEDT—NCLA BEAUTY	61
CHAPTER 8.	CAROLYN KOCHARD AND MEG GREENHALGH PRYDE—BRANDEFY	65
CHAPTER 9.	LAURA MERCIER COSMETICS—LAURA MERCIER COSMETICS	69
CHAPTER 10.	BOBBI BROWN—BOBBI BROWN COSMETICS	75
CHAPTER 11.	WENDE ZOMNIR—URBAN DECAY	83

CHAPTER 12. MARY DILLON—ULTA BEAUTY   93

CHAPTER 13. JACKIE AINA—MAKEUP AND DIVERSITY   99

CHAPTER 14. GREGG RENFREW—BEAUTYCOUNTER   105

CHAPTER 15. LAURA CRONIN—CLEAN-FACED COSMETICS 115

CHAPTER 16. AISHETU DOZIE—BOSSY COSMETICS   119

CHAPTER 17. KAYLEY AND BLAKE MILLER—PAWS

             BEAUTY   123

CHAPTER 18. SHILPI JAIN—SKINVEDA   127

CHAPTER 19. GINAMARIE MCGUIRE—GINAMARIE   133

CHAPTER 20. SHELLY MAGUIRE   135

CHAPTER 21. VANESSA AMAYA—KREIDA COSMETICS   139

CHAPTER 22. CHANTAL DE GREEF—BASIC BEAUTY TOOLS 143

CHAPTER 23. PATRICIA HARTMANN—RUNWAY ROGUE   147

CHAPTER 24. DEBRA JENN—THE YOUTUBE PERSONALITY 151

CHAPTER 25. ANGELICA WHITE—MAKEUP BY ANGELICA   155

CHAPTER 26. CATHERINE ERWIN—LUNATICK

             COSMETIC LABS   159

CHAPTER 27. JOYCE PLATON—HELLO BEAUTY   163

             CONCLUSION   167

             APPENDIX   169

ACKNOWLEDGEMENTS

Growing up, I always wanted to write a book. Never in a million years would I have imagined having the opportunity to publish a book before the time I graduated college. Writing *Makeupreneur: How to Be a Real Self-Starter* has been an amazing opportunity, and I am so grateful for all of the support. Fulfilling this dream would not have been possible without you all. Thank you first and foremost to my family for supporting me every step of the way, always. Thank you Eric Koester, Brian Bies, Sherman Morrison, and Bailee Noella for guiding me throughout this journey, and thank you to everyone who gave me their time for a personal interview, preordered the eBook, paperback, and multiple copies to make publishing possible, helped spread the word about *Makeupreneur: How to Be a Real Self-Starter* to gather amazing momentum, and help me publish a book I am proud of. I am sincerely grateful for all your help.

*Margaret Donato	*Michael Pawula
Eric Koester	Gianna Dragon
Claudia Karwowski	*Michael Donato
*John Donato Jr.	Janine Seliga

Sara Aldape
*Amanda Donato
~Catherine Erwin
~Laura Cronin
Lynne Donato
Eve Donato
~Tawny Garrick
John Donato
Emily Fruehling
~Kayley Miller
Daniel Pawula
Jim Donato
Khadija Baiiche
Matthew Pawula
Jessica Donato
Debra Delia
Wendy Pollacci
Natalie Lupa
Porfirio Fregoso
Melissa Cubert
Joseph Interdonato
Scott Donato

Jacqueline Saviola
Joseph Donato
Kimberly Penninger
~Hayley Ashby
Sandra Sieverson
Jennifer Carvajal
Shannon Faherty
Alexandra Koziol
Nicole Rose
Eileen Faherty
Michelle Donato
Dave Heigl
Magdalena Kubik
Ann Mentone
Theresa Longoria
Carol Gayer
Suzanne Schwartz
Kathy McKenna
Josefina Gomez Karas
Władysław Maciej
Jim Donato
Sophie Matulajtys

INTRODUCTION

———

There's no avoiding the topic that Kylie Jenner is one of the most well-known entrepreneurs in the modern-day beauty industry, one of the most recognizable, but also one of the most controversial figures of our time. If you don't know about Kylie Cosmetics, just do a quick Google search on the company. Kylie is known for being the youngest stepsister of the Kardashian crew and "the youngest self-made billionaire ever," according to *Forbes Magazine.*[1] Self-made may be a stretch, but billionaire is spot on. The media was in an uproar debating whether Kylie is actually self-made. Well, what I do know is that Kylie Jenner has been on reality television since she was a young child, struck a deal with the PacSun clothing line as a teenager, and has numerous paid advertisement opportunities on Instagram. She claims she did not inherit any money, but she does acknowledge having a huge platform and a powerful network. Whether you believe that

———

1   Robehmed, Natalie. 2019. "At 21, Kylie Jenner Becomes the Youngest Self-Made Billionaire Ever." *Forbes.Com.* https://www.forbes.com/sites/natalierobehmed/2019/03/05/at-21-kylie-jenner-becomes-the-youngest-self-made-billionaire-ever/#6df264ce2794.

her position in society helped build a beauty empire or not, her success is one many of us can only dream of.

I am the same age as Kylie Jenner, but being an entrepreneur in the beauty industry is something that has always seemed unattainable to me. I have even been envious at times that she could start up a makeup line with ease just because she wanted to. If only I had the Kardashian-Jenner network and fan base that would make being an entrepreneur a whole lot easier than being in my position of a middle class, young Midwestern girl who loves the idea of being an entrepreneur in the makeup industry but has no idea where to start. It just never appeared realistic to me. I grew up loving makeup. My earliest memory with makeup was running up the stairs of my house, going into my sister's bedroom, and putting a glittery blush all over my face and topping it off with Lip Smacker lip balm. It was the type of makeup that was probably bought from Limited Too or Club Libby Lu at the time. Funny enough, my face broke from whatever was in the glittery makeup, but this in no way stopped me from continuing to rummage through my sister's makeup bag.

A couple years later, I actually had a legitimate reason to start wearing makeup. I began dancing when I was four years old, and every year there was a big dance recital in June that called for photoshoots and flashy makeup. Bold makeup was expected so it could be seen under the blinding lights of the stage. The older you get as a dancer, the more makeup you are expected to wear. This makeup often consisted of blue eyeshadow, bright, rosy blush, and shiny pink lipstick. If you didn't have a quick change between performances, you had just enough time to switch up your costume and touch up your makeup. We weren't expected to have any makeup skill at my dance studio—it was just all about wearing makeup to catch the audience's attention and avoid looking "ghostly," as my dance teacher would call it. I would never be seen with this kind of makeup look today, but it was such a fun memory I had growing up as a dancer.

Basically, being a makeup fanatic was inevitable for me. By the time I was in eighth grade, I was thinking about makeup in new ways. My best friend at the time and I immersed ourselves in YouTube makeup tutorials, learning the basics of applying a complete makeup look. From foundation, concealer, eyeshadow, eyeliner, and mascara to bronzer, blush, lipstick, highlighter, and more, I wanted to use it all. My best friend and I spent hours brainstorming our own dream beauty line, picturing it with black and white packaging for a chic look. I looked up how to make bronzer from cocoa powder, while she looked up containers to package our hypothetical eyeshadows and bronzers in. As great as it sounded, we didn't make much progress after that. I will never forget that day, though, when two fourteen-year-olds had a dream of doing something big.

Seven years later, one thing I do know is that the makeup and beauty industry is bigger than it has ever been before. Makeup brands are sold out in minutes, purchased by both male and female customers. For example, when the $38 highlighter called "Champagne Pop" was put on the market through Sephora, all twenty-five thousand units were sold out online in around twenty minutes.[2] The demand for the newest and greatest makeup is staggering, and I'm not going to lie—when there's a good product on the market, I want to get my hands on it, too. The market in 2018 generated approximately 89.5 billion dollars for makeup products in the United States, and it is expected to grow.[3] But with bright new entrepreneurs, this doesn't mean leading makeup companies need to continue to dominate the industry. The world of social media has allowed anybody a leg in the game. Carli Bybel, Jaclyn Hill, and James Charles are just a few beauty vloggers who made it in the industry just by putting themselves out there.

I had the exciting opportunity to interview self-starters in the beauty industry and look into the lives of other notable names in the makeup business. I realize not every story is the same, and a very small percentage of self-starters have what Kylie Jenner has: a famous family and 132 million followers on Instagram. What we can take from Kylie Jenner, however, is a business model. Just because Kylie has a unique situation doesn't mean we should be discouraged from following a dream of entrepreneurship in the makeup industry: makeupreneurship. In the case of my book, we will look at both makeup and skin care, as skin care is essential as a frequent makeup user. You need a clean and healthy base on which to apply your makeup. We will look at different levels of makeupreneurs and their stories. Being a makeupreneur

---

2   Panych, Sophia. 2019. "We Tried This Universal Highlighter on Every Skin Tone." *Allure*. https://www.allure.com/gallery/becca-highlighter-champagne-pop-makeup-looks.

3   "Topic: Cosmetics Industry in the U.S." 2019. *Www.Statista.Com*. https://www.statista.com/topics/1008/cosmetics-industry/.

can mean many things, and what success is may be different for each person. Each journey is different, but hearing unique stories may encourage and teach you how to become a makeupreneur. Creating a name for yourself in the beauty industry does not need to seem so far-fetched. In my book, we will look at stories of mothers, full-time workers, bloggers, models, makeup artists, and beauty enthusiasts who took a risk one day to start a journey in the makeup industry. By sharing these unique stories, I hope you will find the foundation you need to become a brave makeupreneur!

READ THIS BOOK LIKE A MAKEUPRENEUR

Treat this book like an eyeshadow palette: Pick and choose the colors (chapters) that are best suited for your interests. Below are some suggestions on how to find the right sections for you.

ENTREPRENEURS

This section of the book is perfect to read if you want to look at a diverse group of self-starters in the makeup industry. From tech startups to beauty studios, this first section of the book will give you an idea of what it means to be a makeupreneur in different shapes and forms. These chapters include Chapter 1: Huda Kattan—Huda Beauty, Chapter 2: Hayley Ashby—Beauty and the Bling Studio, Chapter 3: Tawny Garrick—Deluxia Beauty, Chapter 4: Ashley Oporto—KISSME-NOW Products, Chapter 5: LaVonndra "Elle" Johnson—Elle Johnson Co., Chapter 6: Anjali Wrenn—The Beauty Suite,

Chapter 7: Elin Dannerstedt—NCLA Beauty, and Chapter 8: Carolyn Kochard and Meg Greenhalgh Pryde—Brandefy.

HOUSEHOLD NAMES

This section of the book will give you insights into some of the biggest makeup companies in the world. Read about how they were able to transform an idea into a household luxury makeup brand. If you have plans of taking over the beauty industry, these stories may give you suggestions on how to start your makeupreneurship journey. These chapters include Chapter 9: Laura Mercier—Laura Mercier Cosmetics, Chapter 10: Bobbi Brown—Bobbi Brown Cosmetics, Chapter 11: Wende Zomnir—Urban Decay Cosmetics, and Chapter 12: Mary Dillon—Ulta Beauty.

BEAUTY WITH A PURPOSE

This section of the book demonstrates how to simultaneously shed light on a cause while building a makeup empire. If you are passionate about a serious issue, read how to connect that to your love for makeup through various stories of powerful makeupreneurs. These chapters include Chapter 13: Jackie Aina—Makeup and Diversity, Chapter 14: Gregg Renfrew—Beautycounter, Chapter 15: Laura Cronin—Clean-Faced Cosmetics, Chapter 16: Aishetu Dozie—Bossy Cosmetics, and Chapter 17: Kayley and Blake Miller—Paws Beauty.

CLOSE TO HOME

This section of the book shares various stories of self-starters and what in their personal lives influenced them to get into the world of makeup and beauty. If you have a driving force in your life that is influencing you to get into the beauty industry, read this part of the book for inspiration. These chapters include Chapter 18: Shilpi Jain—Skinveda, Chapter 19: Gina Marie McGuire—GINAMARIE, Chapter 20: Shelly Maguire, Chapter 21: Vanessa Amaya—Kreida Cosmetics, Chapter 22: Chantal De Greef—Basic Beauty Tools, and Chapter 23: Patricia Hartmann—Runway Rogue.

SELF-EXPRESSION

This section of the book shares the stories of entrepreneurs in the beauty industry who got started as a way of expressing themselves creatively. Learn how you can channel your inner artist using makeup. These chapters include Chapter 24: Debra Jenn—The YouTube Personality, Chapter 25: Angelica White—Makeup by Angelica, Chapter 26: Catherine Erwin—LunatiCK Cosmetic Labs, and Chapter 27: Joyce Platon—Hello Beauty.

CHAPTER 1:

HUDA KATTAN— HUDA BEAUTY

———

If you consider yourself an average, small-town person, making it big in the world of makeup may seem intimidating to grasp. "Where do I start?" and "How much money do I need?" would be the first of my many questions. You are not alone, and some of the most successful makeupreneurs today felt the same way. If you ever noticed Huda Beauty in your local Sephora, just know that the CEO of Huda Beauty, Huda Kattan, considered herself to be an average, small-town girl. Today, her makeup line is generating $250 million annually in revenue, according to *Forbes Magazine*.[4]

The first time I ever heard of Huda Kattan was only a couple years ago. Generally, she is a newer face in the beauty industry, and she has started to quickly expand her empire into the United States, having already won over the Middle East

———

4   "Huda Kattan." 2019. *Forbes*. https://www.forbes.com/profile/huda-kattan/#1215d68c3cec.

with her line, Huda Beauty. I came across a Facebook reality show about Huda Kattan and her family business that almost reminded me of *Keeping Up with the Kardashians*. I was sucked into the entertaining world of reality television without knowing much about Huda and her makeup empire. Little did I know she was rapidly growing as one of the leading new faces in the makeup industry around the world. If you watch the series, you will get a sneak peek into the business. To familiarize myself with Huda's self-starting roots, I went to her YouTube channel to watch a video in which she tells her life story. I instantly connected with Huda's story.[5] I may have originally thought her life was another Kardashian tale, but I quickly learned she grew up with a lot less fame and fortune, yet she is still climbing her way up the ranks of the makeup industry. Huda Kattan is absolutely a real self-starter.

To my surprise, Huda Kattan is an Iraqi-American woman who was born in Oklahoma and lived in Tennessee, Massachusetts, and even Dubai. Although she did not stay in one place for long, she grew up as a normal American girl. She was living the white picket fence life. Before Huda could even imagine she was going to have a career in makeup, she studied finance in Michigan, thinking working with numbers would satisfy her "nerdy" side. It ended up doing the exact opposite, however. She realized she was a passionate person, but she just needed to find out what she truly was passionate about, and finance was definitely not it.

---

5   Kattan, Huda. "My makeup business story!" YouTube. http://www.youtube.com/watch?v=Vk41RBKVeho (May 05, 2019).

Huda said she was nervously thinking, "What am I going to do with my life?" It's hard being young and having the expectation that you will know what you want to do with the rest of your life by the time you are twenty. I know this feeling well, as I am sitting here in my early twenties already planning out my life story. But one day, a perfect idea sprung about during a Kattan family dinner. Huda's sister, Mona, suggested she should revolve her career around makeup, because she already enjoyed doing it on herself and others. The other women in her family quickly chimed in with positive responses. The men in her family hoped it wasn't just another silly hobby. Boy, did she prove them wrong—big time!

Words of encouragement from the women in her family were all she really needed to hear, because she immediately booked a flight to Los Angeles to take professional makeup courses that would enhance her makeup skills and techniques. Her family provided her with the love and support she needed, which she would soon need much more when she found out she was pregnant. Huda said, "I became a mom, and at the time that was probably the hardest thing. It was unexpected. I wasn't ready. I had this goal in my mind of what I wanted to do and then all of a sudden, I was not able to do those things. I had a baby on my boob and I was trying to blog with one arm all while falling asleep. It was one of the hardest times of my life." She did not follow the linear path she thought she would follow, but her bubbly and positive personality helped her through the hard times. That, and Oprah. Huda smiled and said, "My biggest inspiration has always been Oprah. I love her. I just like that she fights through all difficulties. There's just no way anything is going to stop her, and that's really kind of endearing and nice to hear when you're facing difficulties." Huda took any support she could to fuel her career, whether that be from her family or the icons she looked up to.

If you follow Huda Kattan's life through her vlogs, you'll quickly see she is well-spoken and confident—major tools in becoming a successful entrepreneur of any kind, but especially a makeupreneur. You never hear stories about entrepreneurs who don't believe in themselves. That's because those are the ones who didn't get very far.

Huda didn't know makeup could ever be a career path for her, but makeup and beauty were always important elements in her life growing up. Her earliest memory of using a beauty product was at the age of fourteen. Huda laughed and said, "Being such a hairy person, of course I loved tweezers." At fourteen years old, she was doing her own eyebrows and doing them for her sister and her friends who were eleven years older than her. Huda said, "I just was kind of fascinated with the idea that you can literally transform into somebody else with just one technique. And I love that. Growing up I always felt like an ugly duckling surrounded by beautiful swans." It is almost innate that young girls turn to beauty products to change something they don't like about themselves. Many women feel this way, always wanting to be better and look better. In today's society, as sad as it is, more girls are set up to feel insecure at a young age, as the media portrays perfect photoshopped women with big eyes, long lashes, blinding white teeth, flawless, glowing skin, full lips, and voluminous hair as the ideal woman. Oh, and don't forget a perfect body. It's hard to keep up at this point. But

Huda was able to quickly view makeup as a positive thing. She found it fun and exciting that you could tweak your appearance while enhancing your own personal beauty. At the end of the day, it's about feeling beautiful in your own skin, and that is how Huda connected with makeup. She would do people's makeup for free, because that's how much she enjoyed helping other people feel beautiful. In fashion shows at her high school and then later at her university, she would be the one lending a helping hand in the makeup department. Ultimately, using makeup is great and exciting, but it shouldn't be looked at as a device to fit yourself into society's totally unrealistic standards. It's about loving yourself and feeling confident.

After completing cosmetology school, she was ready to start attracting clients by creating a blog. Her sister encouraged her because Huda was extremely knowledgeable about all things beauty related. Her schedule was hectic, but you can tell by the constant smile on her face she didn't mind, because she truly loved what she was doing. Huda would wake up at 5:00 a.m. and do makeup from 6:00 a.m. until around 4:00 or 5:00 p.m. When she had time at home, she would do her blog posts for the day, then make an appearance at some type of beauty event so she could evolve into a well-known personality throughout the beauty community. "I remember there was a time where for two months I didn't have any days off, and I loved it," Huda explained with a smile. Someone as driven as Huda was meant to be a businesswoman.

Basically, Huda was working around the clock in a state of pure exhaustion, but she had the time of her life doing so. Don't forget—she was also taking care of a baby. Life doesn't slow down for you when times are rough. Huda kept moving forward with her business development. "One of the great things about having a blog too was having a lot of exposure to brands and amazing people," says Huda. The blog allowed brands and new clients to find her, even leading her to a client who happened to be a princess. She found herself doing makeup at a castle for the princess and her sisters. Her social media exposure attracted royal clients, and soon it was leading her business to well-known American celebrities. One celebrity who will always stick in Huda's memory is Eva Longoria, who is still to this day one of her all-time favorite clients. Note to aspiring makeupreneurs: Social media is powerful!

Yes, Huda was starting out her journey with fantastic results, getting the attention of famous figures in society, but in no way was her everyday routine a piece of cake. Money was tight, and despite her finance degree, she wasn't the best at dealing with money. Even today, she struggles with sponsoring brands for money. Huda explained, "I'm not someone who does a lot of pay posts. I felt like for me, it just didn't fit. Sometimes, I will do some sponsored things if they are brands I love and love the products." She will only sponsor products she genuinely supports, which I respect so much in the day and age when social media is filled with influencers promoting products to make some extra cash whether they use it or not. This is misleading. Take reality television stars, for example, who are often seen with top-notch personal trainers and chefs on their reality show, but then advertise appetite suppressant lollipops and skinny teas on Instagram, claiming they "use" these products to keep the weight off. I'm just going to take an educated guess and say these are not the primary reasons behind their near-perfect image. You can Google any reality television star and find products they are advertising on their personal accounts. Huda could have easily taken up offers to promote brands and make quick money for her business, but she decided to put in real time and effort to keep her journey to success real and authentic. As a result, her success did not grow instantly. After three years of dedication and hard work, she was making $1,500 which allowed her to hire a much-needed assistant. All of the money Huda was making ended up going to her assistant.

Blogging was Huda's first priority, but she had to get back into makeup artistry to support her long-term goal of starting her own brand. She didn't have money lying around to start her dream business in an instant. She had to work for it and draw up the help from others. Family can legitimately shape your future, in a positive or negative way. Huda's older sister, Mona, genuinely believed in her sister's talents, encouraging her to learn makeup and start a blog, then later offering a $6,000 investment to start her brand. Now that's unconditional love and support. You can say family contributed a lot to the success of Huda Beauty. With the start of her blog, her family members were her biggest cheerleaders, always reading and commenting on all of her posts even when nobody else was. However, with the positive comes the negative. Her dad was really concerned about Huda's choice to ditch a career in finance. It wasn't the traditional route, so he couldn't imagine a stable career coming from this. "No, dad! One day people are going to see it!" she would yell at her dad. This tension pushed her to be tougher and more organized to demonstrate her hard work ethic to her father. Some of her friends needed some convincing as well. She quickly proved her family wrong, but there were also doubts from the public. Huda revealed, "One of the other struggles I had when starting out was definitely cyberbullying. I had two incidents where I was pretty badly cyberbullied. It was very difficult for me to work." Putting yourself out there comes with judgement. To grow as a makeupreneur, you will need to take risks, and you will have to endure some negative feedback. Unfortunately, having a large audience on social media can lead to bullying that is out of your control. "Ultimately, it did make me strong," Huda said. She took a hard time and turned it into an opportunity for self-growth. She believed in her abilities, and the hateful comments no longer scarred her. This gave her the ultimate push to take her blog to the next level and prove to her dad and her followers that she could and would create the Huda Kattan empire.

It took a full year of blogging to finally see some type of progress with her brand. She saw a girl from Japan comment on her blog. Huda exclaimed, "People around the world are commenting. It's happening!" This single girl from across the world was a catalyst for her to keep pushing forward. Her followers were global, coming from Africa, North America, South America, and elsewhere. Even while her audience was still emerging, she knew her blog was resonating with some people, which further encouraged her to keep creating content. It takes a special type of patience to work at a blog until you grow a constant readership.

While her followers were gradually growing, Huda used her spare time to create her own false eyelashes. She saw a gap in the market. She wanted a specific type of false eyelash that stores weren't selling. So she took matters into her own hands and started to make her own. Everyone she knew loved what she was doing, so naturally she started sharing them with everyone free of charge. Huda's sister saw the potential of her lash creations and knew she could turn this into a legitimate business. She pushed her into getting a manufacturing company to create her eyelashes. Without her sister pushing her into things, she may have never have done anything on her own. Her sister was a vital part of support throughout Huda's success.

Using her makeup skills to pay for some of it, Huda still needed money to keep up with manufacturing the lashes. She made a deal with her sister: If she would invest in her false eyelashes and the business venture didn't make any money, Huda would pay her back and use the fake eyelashes for herself, which was not much of a loss for Huda, as she loved the lashes she created. People may not know how involved Huda was in creating her first line of eyelashes. From the design to the packaging to even the font used on the packaging, Huda was involved in every aspect. She even used a camera in her house to take a picture of her eyes to be used on the packaging.

From there, her first big goal was to convince a Sephora in Dubai to take on her product, since that happened to be the city she was living in at the time. It was a big goal, but that's what she really wanted. Of course, she had to get a lot of rejections in the process of attaining her goal, but she was persistent. Distributors are hesitant to take on new brands for the fear of them not being successful, but after some time, Huda finally managed to find a distributor to make her dream a reality. After being absolutely persistent and arguing over small details up until the last minute, Huda's line was finally launched at a Dubai mall. Before the launch, she even considered pulling out from the deal, because she had a vision, and if the distributors were not going to comply with how she envisioned her eyelashes, it wasn't worth it for her. She said, "If this is not how I see it in my head, it's not happening." Once her eyelash line hit stores in Dubai, Huda said with a huge grin, "It became one of the most purchased products in Sephora Middle East, and since then we've broken those records." This just proves that if you are passionate about something, you should go with your gut feelings.

The memory of the launch is still fresh in her memory. Huda said, "I remember the morning, I got a phone call: 'Hey the lashes are on sale. There's already a lot of people coming. People are excited.' I rushed to Dubai Mall, and I basically stayed in Dubai Mall the whole entire day. I was super emotional, and even now to this day, every launch that we have, before I see everyone's reaction, I cry. I'm not a crier, and literally the floodgates just flow. And I get really emotional about it, because it's so great to see, when you create a product, people react in a way you only hope they do."

What I love about Huda Beauty is that CEO Huda Kattan truly cares. Every day, large corporations are taking over small companies and tarnishing their unique identities. Huda knew what she wanted for her product and made sure it happened. "We really do put our heart and soul into every product," explained Huda, and it shows in the success of the brand thus far. If I am putting money into a cosmetics

28 · MAKEUPRENEUR

company, I want to know the CEO is genuine and wants her line to be perfect. Consumers don't want a subpar product. As makeup consumers, we want the best possible product we can get for our money. When a makeupreneur is just in it for the profit, you can guarantee you are not getting the best product out there. Of course, as an makeupreneur and with any entrepreneur, money is a huge part of measuring your success, but without loving what is going into your product, don't expect anyone else to love it, either.

As Huda's success was becoming evident, her sister Mona said to her, "You know, I've learned a lot from you. One of the things I learned was although you're a very impatient person, when it comes to work, you're very patient and very steadfast, and you constantly push through no matter what the circumstances are." Huda realizes this perseverance is largely why she got her first big break. It was the hardest time of her life to launch a successful product. She even mentions how being a businesswoman was a struggle in itself. Makeup consumerism is dominated by women, but when it comes to the business side of things, it's a different story. But as a woman myself, I believe anyone can become a player in the beauty industry. Being a woman may be an extra hurdle to jump over in the world of entrepreneurship, but the best businesses are the ones run by people who know their products. Can you guess who has had centuries of experience consuming makeup? Women! This is not to say that people like Jeffree Star and James Charles cannot be successful, because men who wear makeup are just as amazing, but it's not like men haven't dominated the makeup industry already—and every other business venture imaginable. If you didn't already know, the CEOs of L'Oréal, Revlon, Estée Lauder, OPI Products, and MAC Cosmetics are a group of six men working together. These are some of the largest beauty companies in the world, but by the look of the CEOs, it doesn't look like any of them have worn makeup a day in their lives. Just saying. Women like Huda Kattan, with a net worth of $610 million, prove a woman can be highly successful as an entrepreneur.

As cheesy as it might sound, Huda explains that to thrive as a makeupreneur you must "not be confined by your own limitations. That is the biggest hurdle holding people back—that they are confined by their own limitations, and that they are only as big as they think they are, and that they are only able to do as much as they think they can." The only thing stopping you is yourself. Being an entrepreneur in the beauty industry may have always seemed far-fetched, but Huda was just a normal girl trying to figure out her life when she realized she was able to build something of her own. Today, Huda Beauty is much more than a lash line. Huda Beauty has expanded into a full-fledged makeup line with lipsticks, eyeshadows, foundations, concealers, highlighters, primers, powders, and application tools. To build and sustain an empire like the one Huda has created, you can bet there were sacrifices along the way.

Huda Kattan's story doesn't sugarcoat anything in her story of becoming a makeupreneur. But it shows how being a makeupreneur can be attainable if you persevere and take full responsibility for your product and how it is marketed to the world. To get where she wanted to be, Huda had to wear multiple hats, including makeup artist, blogger, business-woman, and mom. She didn't start off with significant sums of money. She worked hard for the money, while creating a likeable personality in the beauty community. From her story, it is clear you must have thick skin as a woman in the beauty industry. Success doesn't happen overnight ,and ideally family and friends are the ones who are going to support you throughout your journey. Huda Kattan is the epitome of what I am calling a makeupreneur.

Check out Huda Beauty at https://hudabeauty.com.

CHAPTER 2:

HAYLEY ASHBY—BEAUTY AND THE BLING STUDIO

———

This story is close to home. When I say close to home, I mean it both literally and figuratively. My good friend is one of the coolest and hardest working makeupreneurs I know. She lives two minutes away from me, and her business is only five minutes away. Earlier I mentioned how, when I was in eighth grade, my friend and I would plan out our own makeup line from bronzers and eyeshadows to the packaging and marketing plans. Well, here I am today writing about Hayley Ashby, owner of Beauty and the Bling Beauty Studio, the girl who had a dream of being a makeupreneur with me. I am proud to say she is killing the makeupreneur business in Chicago. Neither of us have produced our own makeup line (yet), but she is, in fact, an entrepreneur in the beauty industry.

Her love for makeup started around the time of seventh or eighth grade. We became best friends around that time, and we were both interested in makeup and becoming good at it. I will never forget when she bought a Bobbi Brown makeup book. The white cover stuck out to me with its bold black and hot pink font. Some of our first and most basic makeup tricks can most likely be traced back to that book. By the time we arrived to high school, she was a regular viewer of makeup tutorials via YouTube, paying special attention to Jaclyn Hill, Kathleen Lights, and Tati Westbrook. I started to trust her to do my makeup for fun occasions, like concerts and homecomings. She would put false eyelashes and glittery eyeshadow on me. Her work was good, and she loved doing it. She was that friend who kept me updated on the best and latest makeup trends. Without her, I would probably be a lot worse at makeup than I am today.

We went to grammar school together, and we even decided to go to the same high school. But by the time we got to our sophomore year, I started to see changes in Hayley. She seemed sad and disinterested in school. This wasn't the Hayley I knew and loved, so I was confused and concerned as her best friend. There was a point during the fall semester when she missed three to four days of school in one week. At a fast-paced school like ours, that was really the equivalent of missing six to eight days. Something was up, and I was slightly offended that she wasn't communicating with me.

After a rare few days of having no contact with her, I sent her a text message asking what was going on. Did I do something wrong? Had I been a bad friend? I got a response soon after. She wasn't happy with her life at our high school and needed a change. She was depressed and anxious, and she didn't know why. She was going through things I couldn't help her with. Change was the next best option for her. Within those days of lost contact, she was actually transferring over to our neighborhood's public school. I still had love for her, but we drifted apart, and I don't blame her for it. She needed time to figure herself out.

Before long, Hayley was making another transition in her life. Even switching high schools did not fill the void she was feeling. Home schooling was her next best option. She was able to finish high school from home much sooner than the rest of the people our age. You might assume college would be the next step in her life, but college is definitely not the path for everyone, and that is completely okay. In fact, Hayley didn't go to college, and she is better than okay. There were two things Hayley knew: how she had no desire to go to college, which was the societal expectation of her, and how much she loved doing makeup. During my senior year of high school, I was contemplating what college to go to and what I wanted to do with my life, and Hayley was already in cosmetology school getting certified to become a professional makeup artist. In retrospect, Hayley was extremely brave to make a change in her life for her own happiness.

Soon Hayley was doing makeup for homecomings, weddings, proms, Halloween, friends, family, and local salons. I was lucky enough to have her do my makeup many times, whether that be for her portfolio samples or for special occasions such as my senior homecoming. I trust her judgement, and when it comes down to it, she will probably be the one doing my makeup for my wedding day. She was already doing great at what she loved, but she knew she could keep expanding her skills to set herself apart from the competition. Hayley was going to expand her craft from not only being a profes-sional makeup artist to also being an esthetician and lash artist. With this new training, Hayley can now give waxes, spray tans, facials, and semipermanent lash extensions. After building up her portfolio, Hayley was rapidly gaining new clients, especially for lash extensions. Business started booming when Hayley began showcasing her lash extension work on social media. She set up shop in her family's basement, where clients would meet her to get all glammed up.

I would be sitting in her comfy lash chair getting my lash extensions done, and I would always ask her what her next big plans were. We would talk about advertising, potential salon locations, and even possibly moving out of state. I always love talking business with her, because it's fun and exciting, as I have a love for the makeup and beauty industry as well. We were two young teenagers not too long ago, sharing ideas for a makeup brand. I try to help her out in any way I can, whether by sharing her posts on social media or recommending her to friends and family. Sometimes she works twelve-hour shifts a day to ensure her clients get the services they need. I love watching her succeed, and I know how hard she works.

In February 2018, she took a huge step as a twenty-year-old and bought her own space for a beauty studio. Only a few minutes away from her house, she found a former law office in Chicago that was perfect to transform into a beauty studio. With the help of anyone she could grab, she tore apart rooms and painted walls. There was a specific theme and aesthetic she envisioned for her business, and she was going to make it happen. As a die-hard Disney fanatic, she knew she had to somehow incorporate her obsession into the name of her businesses and connect it to the beauty studio. This is where her name Beauty and the Bling Beauty Studio came about, representing the fun, girly side of the business with the bling and spinning off *Beauty and the Beast* as a tribute to her love of Disney. The name of Hayley's beauty studio shows a playful side, and so does the interior design. Beauty and the Bling Studio is perfectly decorated with just the right combination of classy and girly. She spoils her customers with a stocked mini fridge and their own personal Keurig coffee maker. Hayley wants her customers to immerse themselves in the full beauty experience.

Now, it is almost impossible to book an appointment with Hayley because her services are in such high demand. Luckily, Hayley has already expanded her business to meet the needs of her customers, who travel all across the Chicagoland area to experience Beauty and the Bling. Several lash artists, estheticians, and a microblading professional have been added to the team and trained by Hayley to keep up the high volume of clients.

Whenever I'm in town, I try to squeeze an appointment in with Hayley because I know she's the best, but also because having lash extensions is a great pick-me-up. They make the makeup application process much easier and instantly make your eyes pop. If you're a makeup user, then you know how much lashes contribute to your final look. It's certainly a confidence booster, and most clients can agree on that. When I get lashes done, I receive compliments from strangers all the time. I even got my mom on board. It's extremely important that you see a professional and credible lash artist like Hayley, because without the right expertise and materials, someone can easily damage your natural eyelashes, which is not what's supposed to happen. Ever. Luckily, as Hayley's eyelash crew is all certified, they can even help to try to reverse the damage they see with some clients. They have seen clients who have botched lashes from going to lash artists who don't have proper training or health standards. Also, certain clients may have eyelash loss from cancer treatments or diseases, and Beauty and the Bling is always happy to help.

As mentioned earlier, her studio is not just about eyelash extensions, even though many of her clients are die-hard fans of her work. It's about the total beauty experience. She started with makeup, and that's something she will never stop doing. At Beauty and the Bling, you can also enjoy facials, tans, waxes, and now microblading services. Microblading is a semipermanent tattooing technique that gives the eyebrow a natural, full look. People may want this done for many reasons, such as having patchy eyebrows or just wanting bolder eyebrows. By incorporating microblading, the studio is meeting a lot of beauty desires of their clients. According to the Art of Beauty, the amount of people getting microblading done has tripled from just 2009 to 2015.[6] It is in demand, and Hayley knew it was necessary to bring it to the studio. Like lashes, microblading simplifies your makeup routine. In addition, the people who want facials and temporary tans are usually the ones who wear makeup, so getting a facial or tan is something Beauty and the Bling offers. On special occasions, Hayley even hosts Botox and filler parties during which a professional comes in and Hayley provides

---

6   "Why Is Microblading Going to Dominate the Beauty Industry in Years to Come?"—*Phibrows USA*—*Art of Beauty Academy.* https://www.artof-beautyacademy.com/microblading-dominates-beauty-industry/.

food and drinks for her guests. You can leave Beauty and the Bling Studio with a shopping list of beauty needs checked off.

I consider Hayley a makeupreneur, even though she has expanded her business into so much more than just makeup. But that's what the best entrepreneurs do: they take over the industry, and in this case, it's the beauty industry in her corner of the world. Another thing setting Hayley apart is how she has become a certified lash instructor. Sign up with her, and you will get all the supplies and skills needed to become a trained lash artist. She wants others to be able to do what she does and thrive just as much. Someone like her could selfishly keep her talents to herself, but there's always a demand in the beauty industry, and her plate is already full. I trust her and her company to make anyone who walks out of there feel beautiful. Hayley loves what she does and wants to make sure every customer is happy. According to the Professional Lash and Brow Artists' Industry survey, 80 percent of lash artists are satisfied or very satisfied with their career. In addition, 63 percent are earning what they expected to.[7] These statistics mirror Hayley's experience with lash artistry.

As Hayley is a close contact of mine, I asked her three questions that I felt would be most important for any future self-starters. First, I asked her what made her initially take that step to have a career in makeup and beauty. Hayley

---

7 "First-Ever Eyelash and Brow Artist-Industry Survey by Glad Lash Inc. Showcases a Highly Trained and Satisfied Group of Professionals." 2019. *Prnewswire.Com*. https://www.prnewswire.com/news-releases/first-ever-eye-lash-and-brow-artist-industry-survey-by-glad-lash-inc-showcases-a-highly-trained-and-satisfied-group-of-professionals-300488842.html.

explained, "Working with people all day was definitely a must. I wanted a job with interaction and being able to talk all day. Also, just seeing with myself how big of a difference makeup, lashes, tans, etc., made with my self-confidence, giving that to other people I thought would be the best thing in the world. I feel lucky that I'm even able to make people feel better about themselves and live their everyday lives happier with just a forty-five-minute appointment." It is no secret that getting all glammed up makes people feel good about themselves, but being the person behind the makeup brush is a special feeling.

Second, I asked her how it felt to be an entrepreneur. She responded, "I get told every day how happy I must be with how great I'm doing at a young age, but being an entrepreneur and owner is definitely not all fun. I love it, but it's definitely one of the hardest jobs you can have. There's constant pressure on you and only you, because you work for yourself and you are now solely responsible to make money and be successful. And if you aren't doing well and making money, then you are the only person to blame, which is a lot on a person. That being said, though, I still wake up every day not believing my life is real, how did everything I wanted to happen, and I now have other people relying on me too for jobs! It's a crazy feeling, but I guess I did something right. Overall, I'm proud of myself, but I always feel like I can keep improving and become bigger and better." She made it clear that before becoming a makeupreneur, you need to be prepared for extreme stress and pressure. Not everyone can handle that. It's your business, so you need to put all the time and energy you possibly can into it. If you don't give it your all, it will show.

Third, I wanted her to give the best advice she could to anyone who wanted to pursue a career in the beauty industry. Hayley started by saying, "There are a lot of bad and selfish people in the beauty industry, and I think that's why you hear a lot of the time, 'Oh, that new salon in Chicago? Yeah, it closed within a year,' or, 'I went to hair school, but I quit.' If you are not passionate about making other people genuinely feel good about themselves and are only in this industry for the money, you will 100 percent fail. You need the mind-set of wanting to help people. I want customers to feel good when they leave my salon. If you don't have that attitude, I guarantee you clients will pick up on it immediately. They can sense fake people and sense the people who do not genuinely care about their clients. Then, they will take their business elsewhere, simple as that. Other than the passion I have for beauty, I'm fully determined to help other girls in the beauty industry. Still to this day, that is my number one goal. I worked for so many awful, selfish people, and I wanted to quit and never see the beauty industry again because it was ugly. Luckily, I found a few good people and found my way. I know so many girls in the beauty industry feel the way I did, and I want to help them and give them a platform to grow and love their job even more. Seeing my employees and now friends grow their clientele, improve their skills, and be excited to work might be the best feeling ever. It is so rewarding knowing I helped them do that. Just be prepared to work the hardest you've ever worked in your life, sacrificing sleep to get to where you want to be in this crazy beauty industry." Like any career, difficult circumstances can happen. Hayley was able to find the right people to work with who uplift their clients and cherish their professional relationships.

From her story, we see that being a makeupreneur means you need to work well with people and always put your best face forward. Also, she shows us that if you take the steps she did, such as getting multiple licenses and certifications to be an esthetician, makeup artist, and lash artist, you can be successful as you grow your skills. I love that Hayley is open about her story. You'll encounter bad people, sleepless nights, and lengthy days, but as long as you love your job and love making others feel beautiful, you were meant to be a makeupreneur.

Check out Beauty and the Bling on Facebook at https://www.facebook.com/Makeupbyhayleyashby.

CHAPTER 3:

TAWNY GARRICK— DELUXIA BEAUTY

———

Makeup brushes are essential for a sharp and clean makeup look. As much you may want to believe, using your hands will not give you the best results. Plus, you're asking for break-outs when you use your hands. Deluxia Beauty sparked my interest with its durable looking and chic makeup brushes. I had the pleasure of chatting with Tawny Garrick, the creator of Deluxia Beauty, as she explained what the company's past, present, and future looks like.

In the beginning phases of starting Deluxia Beauty, just like most beauty enthusiasts, Tawny looked to YouTube for tips, but more specifically, Tawny was looking up YouTube videos targeted at utilizing Amazon.com to sell products. Tawny understood that she could use Amazon's unique platform to evolve her own beauty line. "There are many people who sell random items that have no rhyme or reason per se, but I envisioned and understood that Amazon is an amazing plat-form to launch a brand of my dreams, and if I worked really diligently at launching a product on Amazon and building a basis of multiple products that I held under one blanket brand of my own, it could be so powerful. I started with makeup brushes—cruelty-free—because they were relatively easy to source from suppliers overseas. They are produced quickly, and they do not contain topical chemicals, as I did not want my learning curve to contain topical chemicals and regulations that I wasn't very familiar with in starting out. I started with brushes also because I knew they were a great first product that can be used as a building block to expand with other makeup tools and cosmetics," Tawny said. What better tool to create that makes applying makeup easier and cleaner for makeup users? For makeup and skin care lovers like me, you know it is best to use makeup tools instead of your hands to avoid germs, so brushes are not a bad place to start. Also, with the right brush, the quality of your makeup look can increase greatly.

Deluxia Beauty always has plans of expanding. This means working with a USA manufacturer to create Tawny's visions of actual makeup products in addition to her makeup tools. Eyeshadows, blush, mascara, eyebrow filler, and eyeliner products are on the way. Keeping the manufacturing company in the United States is important to Tawny so she can visit the factory and have total awareness and control of her products. Tawny explained, "It's important to me to showcase and sell the cleanest products I can." The facility Tawny will be using to create her line will not test on animals and will be gluten free and select products will be vegan. A lot of companies we buy from today outsource their products, so it is good to know Tawny wants a US manufacturer so she can control her product.

Tawny is no makeup artist herself, but she lives and breathes makeup. She is the girl who walks into Ulta and Sephora and can't leave without purchasing something. Relatable. I'm a VIP member at both Sephora and Ulta—no, I am not proud of it. She is also the type of girl who proves that you don't need to be an expert at makeup to start your own line. Tawny is currently a successful real estate agent working in Nevada. Her knowledge of business and sales gives her the smarts to be an entrepreneur who handles everything from posting social media content, marketing, and dealing with the administrative side of the business. However, Tawny explains that it is absolutely no walk in the park being a self-starter, especially having a full-time career to begin with. Tawny lists aspects of starting a company that is frankly not sunshine and rainbows: business licensing, permits, taxes, getting a Tax ID number, choosing your brand name, graphic design, social media, photoshoots, sourcing the products, packaging, purchasing barcodes through GS-1. The list goes on. Using the Internet is Tawny's lifeline, and she is constantly using it to make sure she is running her business right.

Although being a makeupreneur is no breeze, Tawny thinks if you are diligent enough to stick to your business plan and execute it, it can be done. In her opinion, the hard work truly does pay off. Tawny enthusiastically said, "But in the end, it feels so worth it, and quite honestly it's the most exciting feeling to look at reviews and receive emails, comments, etc. on how customers feel about your product or can't wait to purchase more!" It is evident that the time and dedication you put into the creation of your beauty line will resonate with consumers. The love and hard work you put into your product shows, and that's coming from a consumer.

With more yet to come for Deluxia Beauty, social media is going to be pivotal in the growth of the company. As Tawny markets her company through social media and gains an abundance of followers, she is going to dabble in public relations and take advantage of the many beauty influencers online. Tawny is also planning on creating YouTube tutorials and doing Q&As to keep in touch with her consumers and never lose sight of their needs. Tawny's experiences show us that you don't need to be an expert in entrepreneurship or a makeup artist to be a makeupreneur. Using the resources available to you through the Internet to learn and grow as an entrepreneur is a huge part of being successful. This is what a self-starter is. She started from ground zero, and soon we will see an extensive amount of growth with Deluxia Beauty.

Check out Deluxia Beauty's Facebook page: https://www.facebook.com/DeluxiaBeauty/.

CHAPTER 4:

ASHLEY OPORTO— KISSMENOW PRODUCTS

———

You may have never seen KISSMENOW PRODUCTS in stores nor ever heard of the makeup line at all, but KISSME-NOW has been seen on eminent faces in the music industry who you certainly have heard of, especially if you are familiar with pop, hip-hop, and R & B music.

Before we get into who has been seen wearing KISSME-NOW, I decided to reach out to the creator of the cosmetics line and see how she got to where she is today. Her name is Ashley Oporto, a twenty-seven-year-old mother to three kids and an avid entrepreneur. Prior to starting her exciting venture into the beauty industry, Ashley and her husband owned a vitamin and supplement shop. That venture was short lived, but Ashley took that experience as a learning opportunity. That was her first time running a business, so now she knew how to go about things differently. For example, she knew her next business would start online before implementing a storefront. Having a storefront can cost around $3,000 a month, compared to running an online store for around $30 a month. After Ashley and her husband's first business venture ended, she decided to stay at home with her kids for the next six years. Without her vitamin shop, she had six years of focusing on her kids, but with no storefront, she had valuable time to spare. In some of that spare time, she would immerse herself in something she enjoyed, which happened to be makeup. She wasn't a makeup artist, or necessarily great at doing makeup, but she was learning. Ashley would jump on people's Facebook live makeup tutorials and see what they were doing. She saw people going live on Facebook as a great marketing strategy that she wanted to be a part of.

Ashley's first product ever made was the KISSMENOW lip scrub, what her brand was first known for. The inspiration behind the lip scrub was her daughter's dry, chapped lips. The perfect formula was made by using natural ingredients you could find at home. She started selling lip scrubs and lip balms on Etsy, where she was able to grow her image. Now she sells false eyelashes, cosmetic glitters, brush sets, eyeliners, an eyeshadow palette, lip balm, and matte liquid lipstick, all on her very own website.

When I asked Ashley how to remain successful in the market, she answered, "Remaining successful in a competitive market such as the beauty community is hard, but the key is releasing new products that the consumer would love! Having great quality products makes the customers trust your brand, which makes them come back and buy again. Staying affordable and offering payment plans helps and can bring in new customers as well, because not everyone can just go on the Internet and purchase what they see, which is why I am so happy we offer Afterpay." Afterpay is gives the customer the incredible opportunity to buy the product cheaply up front and then pay the rest later in small increments. This option comes in handy when you simply can't wait until payday to get your hands on the product. KISSMENOW was the first brand I ever saw using Afterpay, and just now am I finally seeing other makeup brands incorporating the system to keep up with the competition.

Ashley really hopes to grow her brand, and I'd say it's heading in the right direction already. Ashley said, "I want KISSME-NOW to grow so much and I am willing to put the work into become an amazing, fun, positive brand that everyone will absolutely love and trust. I put my trust in God to stay on the right path to lead to success." Her customers already love and trust the brand, but the next step is to build even more momentum.

Now, you are probably wondering who has been wearing KissMeNow. Do the songs "Bodak Yellow" and "Money" ring a bell? Makeup artist, Erika La' Pearl, has been using KISS-MENOW on rapper Cardi B. Specifically, Cardi B's makeup artist is a fan of KISSMENOW's false eyelashes and eyeshadows. Erika has been using KISSMENOW products on both herself and Cardi B in her biggest moments in the spotlight. Cardi B has been seen wearing KISSMENOW on the red carpet and on her Netflix series, *Rhythm and Flow*. Someone as huge as Cardi B wearing Ashley's makeup products is a tremendous accomplishment. Cardi B's makeup artist does not fail to tag the makeup brands she is wearing, giving shoutouts to KISSMENOW accordingly. In addition, singer

Ashanti and YouTube star Rich Lux have been spotted wearing KISSMENOW.

A great piece of advice Ashley gave is to reach out to big makeup artists, influencers, and celebrities on social media. You never know who will get back to you. Asking these influencers to give you a shoutout, wear your product, or simply like your posts online is pivotal in growing your brand in the beauty industry, especially in this day and age when everything is so social media focused. Ashley also explains that you don't need to know it all before starting a business. You will learn as you go. She is learning new things every day and has confidence in her brand. "Stay motivated, do what you love, and have patience. Success will come with all the hard work you put in" is what Ashley lives by as KISSMENOW continues to thrive.

Ashley shows that you don't need to be an expert to run a business. It's a work in progress, and no matter who you are, you can attract influential people to give your business a push.

Check out KISSMENOW PRODUCTS: https://www.kissmenowcosmetics.com/.

CHAPTER 5:

LAVONNDRA "ELLE" JOHNSON—ELLE JOHNSON CO.

———

The makeup and beauty industry has so much potential. It is not confined to the realm of upper-class white women, and now more than ever, we are seeing diverse faces from all facets of life becoming badass makeupreneurs. One boss lady I came across who is making strides in skin care and makeup is LaVonndra "Elle" Johnson. Elle Johnson is the founder of Elle Johnson Co., the luxury botanical skin care line.

According to her interview with Digital Beauty HQ,[8] Elle previously owned her own women's clothing boutique in North Carolina. There, she dealt with a lot of branding and advertising, the part of the job she loved. As Elle is a single mother and businesswoman, being at the boutique all day

---

8   Chang, Ciera, 2019. "As Told By: Lavonndra Elle Johnson-Digital Beauty." *Digital Beauty*. https://digitalbeauty.com/lavonndra-elle-johnson/.

was not ideal for her situation. She wanted to try something new, something exciting. This different and exhilarating path happened to be a skin care line. Elle had always struggled with blackheads and oily skin, so skin care was right up her alley. To take the first steps to create a beauty line, she needed to do thorough research on products and the manufacturing process. When you are starting from scratch, research is key. You may think you know everything about the business venture you are getting involved in, but it never hurts to utilize your best resources. The skin care products she was seeing in the current market were confusing and overwhelming to use, so she knew her skin care line needed to be the exact opposite: simple and approachable. So Elle came up with a three-step regimen that couldn't be any more straightforward. It includes a cleanser, toner, and moisturizer. Simplicity reels in all of the busy people out there who don't have time to take care of themselves. Whether you are a new mom, a nurse, or a CEO of a company, your first priority is not your own health and wellness. With a skin care line as simple and effective as Elle Johnson Co., everyone can take care of their skin. These three steps only take a couple minutes out of your day. I would know, because my skin care routine also consists of these three steps. In addition, she also has a sugar facial polish, a deep cream moisturizer, and a miracle beauty oil if you want to go the extra mile to spoil your skin. Elle is also expanding her brand with some new products. From the looks of it, she will be introducing a lipstick line to Elle Johnson Co., which would be a fun addition to the brand.

Elle Johnson Co. has been able to push its way through the mainstream competition and get noticed beyond Elle's hometown in North Carolina. She said, "As a new brand in a sea of many, you have to figure out how to convert the interest into an actual sale. With so many brands in the industry, I knew from the beginning that I'd have to have something that set me apart and something that connected with my potential customer. I found this through my simple one-two-three step approach and the packaging. I believe that people like pretty things and that your skin care should also be pretty. I wanted to create a product that people would be proud to display. Regarding rewards, my biggest wins would be any press mentions and features. It's a tough industry, and when you're recognized by your peers, it's rewarding to know that you're going in the right direction. Plus, press lends credibility to consumers, and sales increased as a result." Some places Elle Johnson Co. has been featured include Yahoo Lifestyle, BET, *Elle*, and local news stations. In addition, it has been featured in the CEW BeautyInsider, which stands for Cosmetic Executive Women. The renowned beauty guru Wende Zomnir, creator of Urban Decay Cosmetics, even encourages new self-starters to join the CEW organization, as discussed in Wende's chapter. Elle Johnson's recognition in CEW BeautyInsider is a huge deal.

Elle has tackled balancing family and business head on. Up by 5:00 a.m., she handles the tactical end of the business by sending out orders, writing brand placements pitches, and responding to messages. When orders and messages have calmed down, Elle will spend the rest of her day sifting through social media, making noteworthy captions, and scoping out competitors. She tries to end her day by 4:00 p.m. so she can spend time with her daughter and unwind. She even tries to get her daughter involved by having her photograph Elle Johnson Co. products with her. Once her daughter gets older, she will most likely have a larger role in the business.

Digital HQ Beauty captured Elle giving fantastic advice to any future female entrepreneurs in the making. She said, "My advice would be to have tough skin and be ready for all the times you'll hear no, but prepare for that eventual yes. Also, be aware of what's going on within the industry. Take an active role in attending events and putting yourself out there. You should definitely pitch yourself beyond your local market. Ultimately, you have to have the confidence to just go for it." Elle Johnson, a single mother and woman of color, shows us that as long as you're brave and taking initiative in building a brand for yourself, you can make it happen no matter who you are.

Through Lavonndra Elle Johnson's story, we recognize that if you see something lacking in the beauty market, that is a perfect opportunity to create something of your own. Do your research and make things happen. If you're a self-starter with no connections in the makeup industry, it doesn't mean you can't succeed—it just means you'll need to put in the extra work to get recognized by the right people. Go get started.

If you are interested in Elle Johnson Co., here is the website: https://www.ellejohnson.co/.

CHAPTER 6:

ANJALI WRENN—THE BEAUTY SUITE

———

Not everyone is the best at doing their own makeup. Sometimes, you just want a professional you can trust to make you look good and feel good for the day. Once you find the right makeup artist for you, you'll be hiring them to do your makeup for all of the important events in your life: weddings, birthdays, business events, or just because you need a pick-me-up. Recently, I found a makeup artist who takes glamorous to the next level. I was lucky enough to get in contact with lead makeup artist Anjali Wrenn, co-creator and co-owner of the Beauty Suite. The Beauty Suite is an exclusive bridal, beauty, and special event studio located in New York City. From the sounds of it, Anjali is truly living her best life. Anjali, thirty-two-year-old Staten Island native, is happily married to her high school sweetheart and blessed with a twelve-year-old son. Anjali's true loves are her family and her business.

Since Anjali was a little girl, makeup has always sparked her interest. She reminisces about her childhood watching her grandma sit down in front of her vanity every day applying makeup. This little memory remains significant in her life today because she is a powerhouse in the makeup industry. Only ten years ago did Anjali get professionally involved in the beauty industry—hard to believe considering her makeup abilities are captivating. She started as a brand representative and freelance artist for Benefit Cosmetics. From that experience, she was able to attain loyal customers as well as connect with other beauty professionals. After accepting a position at MAC Cosmetics, Anjali's career blossomed. Through MAC, she was able to grow her skills and clientele. A few years later, she decided she had enough clients and connections to build an image apart from MAC or Benefit. Her clientele, which consisted of brides, brides-maids, and women attending special occasions, grew exten-sively as she took on the tristate area. With her business partner, she spent hours brainstorming and envisioning how to create a successful beauty studio. Anjali and her partner officially started their business, the Beauty Suite, in May 2018.

Today, business is booming, and all Anjali's fears of opening a makeup business have vanished. "I am proud to say I have now become one of the most sought after makeup artists in the NY/NJ area, and the Beauty Suite has become the go-to spot for all beauty and glam services in Staten Island, NY," Anjali said. If you go to Anjali's Instagram page, you can see that her work is being sought out by many. Even *Jersey Shore* star and Staten Island native Angelina Pivarnick is a happy customer of the Beauty Suite. Angelina trusted Anjali to do her makeup on her wedding day. Her makeup allowed her to feel confident and beautiful throughout the entire day. Fans of Angelina couldn't help but gush over the way she looked on her big day, thanks to the expertise of Anjali Wrenn. The Beauty Suite goes beyond makeup artistry. It offers professional hair services fit for any occasion. After a client is all glammed up, it offers professional photoshoots to capture the client's look. Also, Anjali collaborates with other notable makeup artists to host a bridal makeup masterclass. The Beauty Suite even hosts events such as children's glam camps and birthday parties.

Anjali's success shows, and I wanted to know how she keeps up in an ever-competitive industry in one of the largest cities in the United States. Well, Anjali was happy to share and said, "I remain successful by waking up every day and pushing myself to do better and work harder no matter how tired or overwhelmed I may be. My success also comes from a strong support system. My partner, husband, mom, and even my son supports me and helps me to be the best I can be. They are all understanding of the long hours and dedication it takes to be a successful business owner, and they are there for me when I need anything. My success can also be attributed to the way I manage all my relationships. I treat my clients, customers, and other industry professionals as if they were my family. I want them to know they will be treated with the utmost respect and care, and I want everyone to leave happy and know they made the right choice choosing me, whether it be for makeup application, their wedding day, photoshoots, or collaborative projects." As a customer, it is comforting to know that a makeup artist like Anjali wants you to feel your best when you are with her.

Getting your makeup done by someone who treats you well and makes you feel good is a huge party of the beauty experience. You want to be comfortable with your makeup artist, not only because you want to enjoy your short time with them, but also because you want to be able to express what you want in a makeup look so there is no miscommunication and it turns out how you want. For example, if you see your makeup artist picking out a lip color that is out of your comfort zone, you want to feel comfortable enough to tell them you would prefer another color. In high school, I got my makeup done for prom, and the artist ended up putting so much makeup on me that I felt uncomfortable in my own skin. My experience is not the type of experience you should have with a makeup artist. If she was more approachable, I would have told her to tone down the makeup a bit.

The one regret Anjali has is not going to college. Anjali said, "I went to college for two years and felt at the time that the career I wanted wasn't something that could be taught in college. I always knew I wanted my career to be one where I could create beauty in some way and didn't realize that there were other majors that I could have taken that would also lead me down that career path." Business degrees and communication degrees are great choices for someone who wants to run a makeup business, but Anjali is still succeeding despite not having a college degree. Also, it is never too late to get one if you think it will benefit you.

Anjali advised "to always be mindful of your reputation and what people say about you after an interaction. It doesn't matter how great your skills are—if people don't feel like they can relate to you and trust you, they won't speak highly of you or refer you to others. Your personality and how you treat people is most important." This advice can be useful in any industry, but especially in the makeup industry, in which you have to put your best face forward, literally and figuratively.

Ultimately, Anjali's story shows us not only how important family and friends are in supporting you throughout your journey, but also how important it is to be a genuine, kind human being. Treating someone the way you would want to be treated seems so cliché and trivial, but if you want to make strong and lasting connections with clients, this is the best way to see results.

Check out the Beauty Suite on Instagram: https://www.instagram.com/thebeautysuiteny/.

CHAPTER 7:

ELIN DANNERSTEDT— NCLA BEAUTY

———

NCLA Beauty is a girly girl's dream. The brand is aesthetically pleasing and affordable compared to most high-end makeup brands. Find NCLA Beauty featured in endless amounts of magazines such as *Nylon, Seventeen, Teen Vogue, Marie Claire, Grazia, Elle, Cosmopolitan, Glamour,* and *Essence.* Nail wraps, nail polish, nail care, lipsticks, and lip care products are what NCLA brings to the table. The brand even collaborates with brands like Hello Kitty, Barbie, Beyoncé, Guess, Nasty Gal, and Disney to keep its image exciting. Products by NCLA beauty can be accessed through Amazon, Birchbox, Riley Rose, Revolve, Dolls Kill, and several other popular boutiques. NCLA Beauty has even caught the attention of celebrities such as Paris Hilton, Solange Knowles, Kendall Jenner, Madonna, Constance Wu, Emily Ratajkowski, Hailey Rhode Bieber, Demi Lovato, and more. If these A-listers are representing NCLA Beauty, the company must be doing something right, and I was determined to find out their secret.

Founder and CEO Elin Dannerstedt was happy to give me details about her wild journey thus far. Elin is of Vietnamese and Swedish descent, born and raised in Brussels. She moved to Los Angeles when she was sixteen years old, with French being her native tongue. It was a major change in her life, but soon she would find her way in the most beauty-driven city in the United States. With this big life change, Elin wanted to channel her energy into something she loved. About ten years ago, Elin and her younger sister, Anh-Thu, came up with NCLA Beauty. However, they did not start with makeup right away.

Elin and her sister found a lack of variety in nail art and wanted to do something to change that. Just like Huda Kattan saw a gap in the false eyelash business, Elin and her sister saw that there was much more you can do to decorate your nails. That's when they came up with nail wraps that stick on top of your nails with fun and eye-catching designs. Nail wraps replace messy nail polish and make changing up your nails much easier. Some of these designs include animal prints, polka dots, palm trees, flowers—you name it. With the amount of variety they offer, there's probably a design that fits your personality. That was just the start, because with the success of the nail wrap idea, the brand grew into what it is today: a hip beauty line that has over three hundred unique products. What makes them makeupreneurs are their beautifully tinted lipsticks, jelly balms, and lip scrubs. Elin and her sister work long hours to maintain the success and growth of NCLA Beauty, but they never fail to enjoy their job while doing so. It's hard not to have fun when Elin and her sister are constantly collaborating with popular brands and fun colors and flavors.

Elin and her sister have clearly had great success thus far, so their journey has not involved much regret. However, Elin said, "I try not to look back because it made me who I am today, but perhaps if I had to change something, I would try to make more time to meet people and network. It's amazing what you can learn from others!" Learning from others to get yourself from point A to B is not shameful.

Lastly, Elin ended with some advice for the dreamers out there. She said, "My advice might seem corny, but it's to never give up. Success takes hard work, and you will have major ups and downs, and you must be ready for that. Do not let anyone bring you down from your dreams! Nothing comes easy, and teach yourself habits that will lead you to succeed. Listen and never stop learning!" As cheesy as she might think it is, it is advice that is worth listening to.

To explore what NCLA Beauty has to offer, click this link: https://nclabeauty.com/.

CHAPTER 8:

CAROLYN KOCHARD AND MEG GREENHALGH PRYDE—BRANDEFY

Makeup artists to beauty podcasters to makeup salon owners to beauty chemists are all considered makeupreneurs in my book. Makeup and entrepreneurship have no boundaries, which is so fascinating. You can take your background in communication, business, psychology, computer science, chemistry, art, or no degree at all to make something out of yourself with makeup as your core focus.

I had the awesome opportunity to speak to various makeupreneurs who are quite unique. But first, get on your phone and go to the app store. Search "Brandefy" and download it. Brandefy is a free app that caters to all makeup consumers, beginners and professionals alike. The app was created by Carolyn Kochard and Meg Greenhalgh Pryde, and I was able to get insights into their journey with makeup. Carolyn is a dog lover, former teacher, and wine enthusiast, originally from Florida and now residing in Virginia. When Carolyn would come home from work, she would blog about value brand products for Brandefy, which wasn't in the app form it is today. Meg grew up with a family of entrepreneurs on a farm in Berryville, Virginia, where she spent the early part of her career in category management at a major manufacturer and then worked for a tech start-up until 2016. In 2018, she graduated from the Darden School of Business at the University of Virginia, where she first pitched the idea for Brandefy.

According to the creators, this is how Brandefy works: "Let's say you're tired of spending $60 on your favorite foundation. You want a cheaper alternative, but you want it to perform similarly to the prestige brand. Open up the Brandefy app— or visit the website—and search for that foundation. We'll show you how the drugstore dupe compares to the cult favorite. We compare ingredients, have makeup mavens review the two products side by side, and report on factors like cruelty-free. We aim to help shoppers save money and outsmart marketers." As I scroll through the app, I see categories for face, eyes, lips, cheeks, makeup tools, personal care, hair care, and skin care. The Brandefy app not only covers all your beauty needs, but also your financial situation. The point of a dupe is to save you money while getting the same quality product as a high-end brand. I feel like a kid in a candy store when shopping for makeup, but sometimes it's not in my budget to splurge on whatever makeup I want. With Brandefy, I can still get what I want. For example, makeup fanatics are raving about Tatcha's silk canvas primer. Tatcha is selling its famous primer for $52.

Brandefy offers a beauty expert dupe from e.l.f. Cosmetics. e.l.f. sells a poreless putty primer for only $8. This is a huge difference in price, and surprisingly e.l.f.'s quality is just as good as Tatcha's.

At first, I thought creating an app dedicated to makeup seemed far-fetched for just anybody, but then I quickly realized it is a doable process. Carolyn and Meg started out with a blog, and anyone can get a website made. You can even have a blog or vlog for free on websites like Tumblr and YouTube. Brandefy gained traction as a blog, and Carolyn and Meg realized it would be great in an app form. It all started with an idea. Then getting the app created was the next step. They had to hire a software engineer to create the app that would be downloadable to people's smart devices. Their app had to be tweaked, adapted, and tested until their visions became a reality. Even today, when new features are added to the app, tweaking, adapting, and testing is essential. Carolyn and Meg had a practical idea that they transformed into a business.

I asked Carolyn how they remain successful, and she told me, "We listen to what our users want. They can request comparisons directly in the app, we respond to their messages, and we keep our eyes on trends." The point behind Brandefy is to help customers out, so of course Carolyn and Meg are going to listen to their users.

Carolyn and Meg's journey shows us that if you are listening to the wants and needs of consumers, you too can be a makeupreneur. Carolyn and Meg never once stated they are makeup artists or want to own a makeup line, but what they did do is create an app that allows makeup users to find less expensive alternatives to high-end brands. Our pockets will thank them later.

Check out Brandefy here: https://www.brandefy.info/.

CHAPTER 9:

LAURA MERCIER COSMETICS—LAURA MERCIER COSMETICS

A staple in my makeup routine is Laura Mercier's translucent setting powder. Her translucent powder has been in my makeup routine for several years, and anyone who keeps up with the latest trends in makeup knows that her setting powders are one of the absolute best. It is one of the simplest makeup items, but to me and many others, it is the most important part of a finished makeup look. I personally use it to control shine and oil, but it can also be used to "bake," which is when you leave the translucent powder on your face for a minute or two so it brightens your makeup and keeps it in place. Looking back, one of my first memories of shopping at Sephora was seeing Laura Mercier's tinted moisturizer on display. The tinted moisturizer is just as successful years later, so she must be doing something right.

According to the *Forbes* article "Why the $445 Billion Beauty Industry Is A Gold Mine For Self-Made Women," about forty prominent makeup start-ups were created by women, with Laura Mercier being one of them.[9] Makeup is primarily used by women, and that cannot be denied. Only forty brands that are well-known are created by women? Seriously? With the infinite amount of makeup brands that already exist, the math doesn't seem to add up. Logically, you'd expect women to be the ones leading the beauty industry since the beginning of time. Of course, throughout history, women have had constant hurdles to overcome, but today there's no excuse for a woman to not be taken seriously in the makeup industry. If anything, I'd trust a passionate, makeup-loving woman to steer the beauty industry in the right direction. Laura Mercier has been a main player in the makeup industry for over twenty years, so hearing her story can give us insight on how to create and withhold a strong business in a competitive industry.

To further understand Mercier's journey, I came across a *Forbes* interview with Karin Eldor and Laura Mercier. I found out that Mercier is a French-born woman who moved to Paris to study painting and art. Unless you're the next van Gogh or da Vinci, an art degree doesn't guarantee financial security. At the end of the day, bills needed to be paid, so she attended the Carita Beauty Institute, where she immersed

---

9   Eldor, Karin. 2018. "How Laura Mercier Has Remained a Force in Beauty, After More Than 20 Years." *Forbes.Com*. https://www.forbes.com/sites/karineldor/2018/09/30/how-laura-mercier-has-remained-a-force-in-beauty-more-than-20-years-later/#676da23258fa.

herself in skin care and makeup application. After she earned her credentials, she decided to move to New York City, which is notably a city full of life, fashion, and art: a perfect combination for an aspiring makeup artist. New York was full of opportunities for Laura. She worked for *Elle, Allure, InStyle,* and *Glamour,* all magazines that appreciate the latest trends in makeup. Her work even extends to celebrities such as Julia Roberts, Sarah Jessica Parker, Mariah Carey, and Madonna. She was even one of the main makeup artists for *Vogue* photoshoots for ten years. The best thing about being a makeup artist is that if you're really great at what you do, word of mouth will quickly spread your name. Ultimately, her exposure to high-end fashion and makeup was a perfect tool to start a company of her own.

Laura Mercier's roots influenced the creation of her beauty line. With a French vibe and mindfulness of art, she created her line in 1996. "What makes you unique makes you beautiful" is the core message of her company. Many years later, her message still resonates with people. Today, Laura Mercier Cosmetics is earning an estimated $2.6 million in revenue annually, according to Owler.[10] This may not be as much as other high-end brands, such as BECCA Cosmetics earning around $10 million annually, but Laura Mercier remains an iconic makeup brand throughout the world.

Karin Eldor of *Forbes Magazine* asked Mercier how she handled founding the company. Mercier claims she barely had time to think about it because she was constantly coming up

---

10   "Laura Mercier Competitors, Revenue, Number of Employees, Funding and Acquisitions." 2019. *Owler.* https://www.owler.com/company/lauramercier.

with new creations at a fast pace. She was too busy being a perfectionist to actually think about what was going on. Basically, her type A personality took control during the start-up. The success of her makeup line was accelerating quickly, and she could barely take a moment to notice it. Laura Mercier's beauty line is about twenty-three years strong and has lived through a lot of change in the industry since then. She recognizes that François Nars and Bobbi Brown were pivotal in the growth of the makeup industry. Like Bobbi Brown influenced Laura Mercier, the prominent companies of today can inspire us to make our own strides in the world of beauty. Laura said, "These lines helped change the mentality of the cosmetics industry, in my opinion, because the big brands were looking at us like we were mosquitoes nagging them, but at the same time, they realized that we were quite right in what we were proposing to clients. So, I think we—the makeup artist brands—became the focal point of attention for a lot of big brands. And from then on, more and more people have been starting their own beauty brands today, independently." Laura recognizes the importance of being an independent self-starter. Our beauty needs cannot always be met by the large makeup corporations, often ran by non-makeup using men.

Karin Eldor asked Laura the question we have all been waiting for: What are your three biggest tips for female entrepreneurs looking to start their own company? Laura generously shared her insight for all the future female makeupreneurs.

Laura breaks it down:

1. "Have passion for what you do, something you authentically believe in, rather than thinking, 'I'm going to create something because it's going to make a lot of profit.'

2. The importance of quality when it comes to everything related to the product(s): from service to the ingredients and formula, etc. Of course, you have to be a good business person, because you don't want to invest too much money and then not make enough. It's just that you have to balance both, to be able to authentically give your client something that you believe is a very good product. Otherwise it will not go very far.

3. Good management, business-wise. You don't want to lie to your client and you don't want to sell garbage; you want to be a person who is recognized for being honest in offering a great product. Good management also relates to your team and people, because ultimately your team is either making the product or selling the product."

If you don't know where to find inspiration when trying to be a makeupreneur, Laura tries to soak up inspiration from every aspect of life. Nature, music, movies, and people have all been sources of inspiration for Laura. My own visions of a hypothetical makeup line come from movies and music. There is so much to work with, and it is all around us. Sometimes, we forget our inspiration can be found right in the center of our lives. Laura was introduced to the book *The Road Less Traveled* by M. Scott Peck, and that has inspired her and allowed her to rethink her attitudes. She even thinks this book helped open up new career paths. Everyone finds motivation and inspiration in different places, but it's important that you do indeed find it.

Laura Mercier's story is a great one to remember, as we can incorporate some of her successes into our own makeupreneurship journeys. First, get to know makeup, whether that be professionally or for fun. Money is huge, but you need to be passionate about your product. Your product can't be subpar with all of the competition out there. It needs to be high quality, and today it will be even more appreciated if it's ethically sourced. Find the right business partner who's going to help you succeed and not bring you down creatively. Finally, channel things that inspire your love for makeup, and you'll quickly be named a makeupreneur.

Check out Laura Mercier's official website: https://www.lauramercier.com/.

CHAPTER 10:

BOBBI BROWN—BOBBI BROWN COSMETICS

———

One of my first encounters with a professional, high-end makeup line was seeing my friend's *Bobbi Brown Makeup Manual: For Everyone from Beginner to Pro.* It is a makeup guide loved by many because it can be utilized by beginners and professional makeup artists alike. Since Bobbi Brown was one of my earliest memories of a high-end makeup brand, I thought I would look into her story to see how she made it as one of the most well-known and consistent makeupreneurs of our time.

I got to explore the professional journey of Bobbi Brown through an *Inc.* magazine interview. *Inc.* specializes in small businesses and startup companies, and Bobbi Brown was a perfect fit, because before she became a household makeup name, she started off small.[11] The interview was done by Bobbi herself but told by Athena Schindelheim. Bobbi Brown started off the interview by explaining exactly why she started to use makeup, and unfortunately, it's a reason a lot of women start to wear makeup: insecurities. Bobbi just wanted to fit in and look pretty. It's a common theme for women on their journey toward self-love. Bobbi wasn't trying to cake on lots of makeup just because she was insecure. She tried to emulate Ali MacGraw in the 1970 movie *Love Story*. Ali MacGraw, also known as actress Jenny Cavilleri, is a natural beauty who appears to be wearing very little makeup. Something I've seen in myself and in other women is that just because you may wear makeup at times to feel better about yourself, it doesn't have to be seen as entirely negative. You can use makeup as a tool to grow your confidence. Confidence levels fluctuate at random times in a woman's life and makeup might just be the right pick-me-up to feel good. For example, often, new mothers who just had a baby feel unattractive and not their best selves for a while. It's a thing to get a "mommy makeover," in which the new mother gets a new hairstyle and their makeup done. It's all about feeling fresh and pretty, and nothing is wrong with that.

Bobbi spent a year at the University of Arizona and six months at the University of Wisconsin trying to find herself in college as many of us try to do. She told her mom she felt like she needed to remove herself from college because what she was doing wasn't going to make her happy in the long

---

11   Brown, Bobbi. 2007. "How I Did it: Bobbi Brown, Founder and CEO, Bobbi Brown Cosmetics." *Inc.*, 2007. https://www.inc.com/magazine/20071101/how-i-did-it-bobbi-brown-founder-and-ceo-bobbi-brown.html.

term. Her mom responded, "Pretend today is your birthday and you could do anything you want." Bobbi said, "I would love to go to Marshall Field's and play with makeup." With that specific answer, Bobbi's mom knew there was a different plan for her. That's when Bobbi's mom suggested doing theatrical makeup in college. Third time's the charm—Bobbi started at Emerson College in Boston. There Bobbi found her place in school and knew she was meant to be doing makeup.

Bobbi never once had a doubt in her mind that she wouldn't be able to succeed, and maybe that's what we can learn from her. She moved to New York City, unpacked her bags, and looked up makeup, photographers, and modeling agencies in the phone book. Her makeup portfolio was from the work she did in college—mostly using her own face as the canvas. This was all during the 1980s when makeup was extreme. The '80s were a time when more colorful makeup was in style. Icons were seen with pink, purple, silver, red, and blue makeup on. That may have been the trend of makeup at the time, but Bobbi wasn't impressed. She was really drawn to the simple and natural look, the look that Jenny Cavilleri embodied in *Love Story*. Today, Bobbi realizes she was a driving force in making natural makeup popular.

In 1988, Bobbi Brown found herself doing makeup for a *Mademoiselle* photoshoot. Then one day, Bobbi and her crew were exploring cool places in the city and ended up in a Kiehl's pharmacy, where she began chatting with one of the chemists. Bobbi told the chemist what she wanted in a lipstick. She wanted a creamy, long lasting, odorless, and natural-colored lipstick, which was unlike the current lipsticks on the market. He offered to make Bobbi her ideal lipstick.

She mixed a taupe colored eye pencil and a blush together to get the desired swatch color ready for him. She called it "Brown," and it later became her number one selling lipstick. That's how her makeup line got started. People often forget that to create makeup, you will need to consult with a chemist or chemistry lab that can make your vision come to life.

Bobbi's vision relied on simplicity. "Wow. If I could make a collection of ten colors, I can't imagine a woman needing any other color," Bobbi stated. She was tired of seeing lip colors that blinded everyone in the room. Simple was better in her opinion, and I know a lot of people who would agree with her. Colors that appeared like it could be somebody's actual lip color and colors that accentuate your lips and match with your every outfit is what Bobbi was going for.

Bobbi was onto something, and it was catching on quickly. It turns out not everyone in the '80s wanted that electrifying makeup look. A *Glamour* beauty editor featured Bobbi in about three lines of the magazine and, although short, that coverage ignited her business. Bobbi was flooded with orders. It was time for her to make her lipstick creations more official because of this unexpected demand. Rosalind Landis, a woman who had hired Bobbi at her PR firm to talk about how to use eyeshadow, would become vital in Bobbi's cosmetics line. Bobbi and her husband and Rosalind and her husband put $10,000 together to officially create Bobbi's company: Bobbi Brown Cosmetics.

Socializing with the right people is essential in any industry. I hear it all the time as a college student: "Networking is key. It's all about who you know." Knowing the right people has always been the key to success in business, and I see that more and more every day. A lot of the success I've had already has been because I have been able to connect with the right people. It's really amazing what being open to connecting with people can do for you. Keep meeting people. Keep your eyes and ears open. Bobbi Brown escalated her business to the next level by keeping conversation at a dinner party. Bobbi asked the woman near her, "What do you?" By fate, or just by pure luck, she responded, "I'm the cosmetics buyer at Bergdorf Goodman." Wow, now Bobbi was definitely at the right place at the right time. Either the cosmetics buyer at Bergdorf Goodman really believed in Bobbi's makeup line, or she just wanted to be personable. She said to Bobbi, "We have to take them," in response to hearing about Bobbi Brown lipsticks. Imagine how amazing it would be to hear those words as a fresh, new makeupreneur just starting out. That amazing feeling quickly vanished, however, when she reached out to them after the party. The buyers at Bergdorf's told her there was already too much going on in the current makeup season, and they would have to pass on Bobbi Brown Cosmetics entering their stores. As gut-wrenching as that may be, Bobbi wasn't going to stop pushing forward. Shortly after the rejection from Bergdorf's, Bobbi was doing makeup for a Saks Fifth Avenue photo shoot, during which she was chatting away about her makeup business. The creative and art directors quickly told Bobbi that they wanted them at Saks stores, too. Now another huge department store was intrigued by Bobbi Brown Cosmetics. So Bobbi made a point of calling the buyer at Bergdorf Goodman back to respond to their previous message about not wanting Bobbi Brown Cosmetics in stores. Bobbi called and said, "That's too bad, but don't worry, because Saks wants it." Finding out the competition was already onto Bobbi Brown cosmetics didn't sit well with the buyer of Bergdorf's. She called back within ten minutes stating they wanted to bring her makeup into Bergdorf stores. Bobbi took the deal, because Saks didn't actually make an official deal yet. It just pushed Bergdorf's to take the ultimate risk.

Once her brand was hitting stores, customers were already sold on her natural colored lipsticks, and they were ready for her to come out with more products. She was being treated like a celebrity. She was being asked to do photo shoots, but not in the way she was accustomed to. She was actually the one featured now. Next, she was quoted for things in magazines that went beyond the scope of makeup. Things were on an upward spiral, and she couldn't believe it.

Her success was a threat to the big guys in the makeup industry, so much s, that Leonard Lauder, chairman of Estée Lauder, was ready to purchase Bobbi Brown Cosmetics. Looking out of his balcony peering into Central Park, he said to Bobbi, "We want to buy you because you are beating us in all the stores, and what you've done is amazing, and you remind me of my mother when she started." That's a huge compliment when an iconic competitor is intimidated by you. Bobbi took the deal because the opportunity was compelling. I'm sure they gave her a deal that was impossible to decline. After the deal was finalized, Estée Lauder would be able to expand Bobbi Brown Cosmetics globally because of all of their connections Bobbi Brown Cosmetics didn't have access to. They would keep Bobbi in her current role, because what she was doing proved successful already. Rosalind joined the merger as well by working with Estée Lauder's corporate office, though she eventually parted ways.

Business with Estée Lauder was a bit shaky for a while. Bobbi Brown items were being knocked off and named "Essentially Brown." So Bobbi met with the Estée Lauder CEO to talk about the way business was being conducted around her line. He told her she wasn't setting herself apart from other companies. She knew how to fix the problem immediately. Bobbi said, "You want to know what I would do? First of all, move out of the GM Building. Move downtown into a cool loft. Put in my head of marketing, Maureen Case, as president. And completely open, change the culture." And that's exactly what happened, improvements and all. Bobbi Brown Cosmetics was taking on a fresher and lighter vibe with editorial photographs and smashed lipstick advertising. By 2006, the company hit half a billion dollars. Today, Bobbi Brown Cosmetics is still relevant as ever. By being confident in her vision, and with constant networking and finessing, Bobbi became an iconic makeupreneur.

Bobbi's story shows us that just because everyone else is following a certain trend—like '80s makeup—doesn't mean you need to settle. Wear makeup that speaks to you, and if you can't already find it, go create your own. She also spent a lot of time mingling with people. Tell the right people about your business ventures because they might be able to take your career to the next level.

Check out the official website at: https://www.bobbibrown-cosmetics.com/.

CHAPTER 11:

WENDE ZOMNIR— URBAN DECAY

———

Urban Decay is one of the spunkiest brands out there. From a Gwen Stefani collaboration to a *Game of Thrones* collection, you know Urban Decay is badass. Within the Urban Decay brand, you will find everything you could want and more. I have purchased the Gwen Stefani eyeshadow palette, the All Nighter makeup setting sprays, Urban Decay Naked Skin concealers, foundations, eyelid primers, eyeliner, blushes, bronzers, and the Urban Decay Naked2 and Naked3 eyeshadow palettes. Okay, I guess you could say I am a fan. Before I reminisced on all of my Urban Decay purchases, I never really realized how much of a loyal customer I am. Then, after listening to an ABC podcast with host Rebecca Jarvis and Wende Zomnir, the founder of Urban Decay, I became an even bigger fan. Wende has grown Urban Decay into a household name that pushes the boundaries of basic makeup. In "No Limits with Rebecca Jarvis," she interviews women who have built an extraordinary empire for themselves, including Wende Zomnir, makeupreneur of Urban Decay.[12]

Wende Zomnir has pushed the boundaries of makeup ever since she was young. Growing up, Wende lived in Texas for a while, where she apparently pushed the limits too far, because she got sent home from school for wearing too much eyeshadow. Wende even said that if she's wearing too much makeup in Texas, home of pageant queens and debutantes, that's saying a lot. Now as an esteemed business owner of a globally known makeup brand, she said, "And even now I feel like it's a little bit of sweet revenge with this whole Makeup Revolution that's happening. When I first started, you know, I came out here to New York and had all my makeup on, and people looked at me like I was bananas. And now it's come full circle where I feel like I don't wear any." Ironically for Wende today, the makeup industry has grown to embrace dark, bold, and colorful makeup. Colorful makeup is praised today, but when Wende was trying to be rebellious with makeup, it was looked down upon. Today, nobody bats an eye if you wear blue eyeliner and orange lipstick. Another thing that has contributed to the makeup revolution, as Wende calls it, are social media platforms and beauty influencers. Without them, customers would be forced to go to makeup counters in department stores from the makeup companies that have always had the most power, such as Estée Lauder. Now indie brands are able to grow and have a fighting chance in the market, which is vital for self-starters.

---

12   ABC. 2017. "#3 Wende Zomnir, Urban Decay." Podcast. No Limits With Rebecca Jarvis.

Before Urban Decay was born, Wende was a scuba diving instructor, a surfer girl living in Laguna Beach. She even had offers to teach scuba diving in Hawaii. It clearly doesn't matter what you do prior—you can be an entrepreneur in the makeup industry if you really want to be. So Wende strayed from the surfer girl life when she met Sandy Learner, the co-founder of Cisco Systems, a leading networking hardware company in the United States. Sandy was a wealthy businesswoman who also shared a passion for colorful makeup, but there was no good quality makeup that explored fun colors like blue, green, and purple. Instead, the market was full of the typical basic pinks and nudes, which are great, but it's not much to work with for people with an edgier side. Wende expressed herself through makeup and broke the norm on what a full face of makeup should look like. Wende explained, "To me it was all about self-expression, and not about following roles. And when I met with Sandy, she had this vision as well. So it was a really cool meeting of the minds, and Urban Decay was born." Just because of a simple conversation, Wende came up with the idea behind the business. Wende's scuba diving job allowed her to talk to new people every day, and Sandy Learner happened to be the right person to push her mind into business mode.

What primarily got Urban Decay into stores was nail polish, similar to how Elin and Anh-Thu Dannerstedt came up with the idea for nail wraps before they started creating makeup. Wende started creating nail polish on her own in a tiny apartment. Wende made a decent nail polish, but the process of getting into stores wasn't that straightforward. Her boyfriend had a friend visiting the apartment who was selling swimsuit wraps to big-name stores. She knew he was calling a Nordstrom, so while he was in the shower, Wende pulled out his buyer list, wrote down important names and numbers, then quickly put the sheet back. This was sneaky, but she knew how important a contact like this would be for her. She picked up the phone and got to work. With a little metal box from Ikea full of samples, Wende pitched Urban Decay cosmetics to Nordstrom once they agreed to meet with her. She got the buyers interested, but now she had to figure out how to deliver what she promised to provide. Thankfully for Wende, Nordstrom bought regionally, so getting orders out in time was doable. Slowly but surely, Urban Decay started selling to more regions. Starting with one region at a time allowed the Urban Decay team to be prepared for expansion in the future. Starting slowly helps with cash flow issues, especially for a new business.

Sephora's expansion beyond France and move into the United States was a win-win for both Sephora and Urban Decay. Sephora needed new bright makeupreneurs in the United States, and Urban Decay wanted to grow its business even more. Wende truly believes that the growth of Sephora allowed Urban Decay to grow right alongside them. As mentioned earlier, department stores were the gatekeepers of the beauty industry. Counter workers like you still see today at department stores would gain the attention of customers strolling by. Now stores like Sephora and Ulta have transformed the beauty buying experience. The customers find the products they want on their own time. They can test out the products and have the employees help them find the right product for them. When I go to Sephora or Ulta, I can always count on an employee to find the right foundation for my skin type and then give me various suggestions on different types of makeup I want to try out. Wende still appreciates her partners at department stores, however. Plus, they have also evolved as well. In short, Urban Decay knew there were people out there who wanted to purchase bright and bold colored makeup, so Wende made it happen, and Nordstrom and Sephora gave the brand a fighting chance.

When Rebecca Jarvis asked Wende what it took to get to where she is today, Wende responded, "It took a village. I definitely have a lot of great people and an amazing team that have all joined in. And it's one big family. I think so many of our key people that run different areas of the business have been there over ten years, so it says a lot about the culture. And it's a very much of a family atmosphere." Wende made it happen, but she recognizes that she didn't do it alone. Her team stuck by her side through it all, and that proved monumental for the company's growth.

What I love the most about Urban Decay is that it embraces uniqueness. Wende said, "Just because you love beauty doesn't mean you want to look like a beauty queen, you know? And maybe you do and maybe you don't, but it should be your choice. And that's what we've always said from the beginning, is its makeup about self-expression. It's makeup for boys and girls. It's makeup for anyone who wants to tell the world who they are. And that's what I always say. It's not about covering your flaws. It's really about telling the world who you are." This is something many people need to be reminded of. Makeup can be a tool of expression, and many makeup users love to express their inner goth, grunge, or punk rock self.

During the podcast, Rebecca Jarvis asks for even more concrete advice on how to really create a successful business in makeup. It was summed up in three key parts:

First, Wende believes having a great business partner leads to great things. She said, "Well, I would say probably the number one thing I really believed when I started this brand was that if you just make great product, and it's creative, and it's good quality, people will find it and they will buy it. And that is not true. You really have to have a great infrastructure. You have to have a great business partner." With the right amount of money, anyone can get quality makeup created. The amount of cool and fun makeup brands out there are endless, but that alone will not be enough. Having a strong infrastructure with a compatible business partner was crucial. For her, that was Tim Warner. He is the CEO of Urban Decay and empowers Wende's creative decisions for the company, while he works on the sales and finance end of the company.

Second to having an amazing business partner is selling to retailers that allow customers to pick up and play with your products. Sephora and Ulta are known for allowing their customers to test out the makeup, but now bigger department stores like Macy's have gotten on the bandwagon of letting the customers take the lead. This way, the customers can find out for themselves how good your makeup products truly are.

The third piece of information Wende shared was about getting over that initial mountain. Once you gain some traction and start hitting sales goals, you will be able to transform your brand with your creative desires. Once you get the money you need, you are able to launch marketing programs and advertisements that will get the brand noticed even more. Your sales strategy is dire because people can easily get into trouble with cash flow, Wende said. If your business is not growing, she suggests really evaluating your business plan and making it strong. That's when having a business partner with financial experience and good investors really comes in handy.

Deeper into the interview, Rebecca Jarvis did not shy away from asking Wende Zomnir how she felt starting out as a woman in a male-dominated industry. This is important to know, as most future makeupreneurs are women. Men have ironically controlled industries targeted at women throughout history, especially makeup. Wende acknowledges that the bigger companies that have been around for years and years are run by men. Look at the CEOs of L'Oréal, Revlon, Estée Lauder, OPI Nail Polish, and MAC Cosmetics. Six men jointly run the $50 billion beauty industry. Unfortunately, a lot of information can be found on the Internet claiming that they are only concerned about cheapening up the production costs so they can maximize profits. This is disregarding the harsh ingredients that are directly soaking into our skin from the makeup.

On the other hand, men have made some great makeup brands using healthy and organic ingredients that nourish and protect our skin. However, Wende pointed out two things about smaller companies. She said, "We see a lot more women and smaller companies having a bigger role. And I think now you see quite a lot of men who actually just want to wear makeup and begin the industry, which I think is really cool." I have personally seen that from the makeupreneurs I have interviewed. These women want the best quality product out there, often keeping in mind eco-friendly, chemical-free, and animal cruelty-free ingredients. This is a time when women are finally being recognized for their capabilities, including being a businesswoman. In addition, some men are expressing themselves through makeup. Society is evolving. The men who own makeup companies should be the ones who appreciate and love makeup. Wende has had suggestions brought to her about making a makeup line for men. But she knows a man who wants to wear makeup wants the real deal, not some alternative.

Finally, Wende Zomnir mentioned an organization called Cosmetic Executive Women. She recommends joining the group via its website if you are looking to get into the cosmetic industry. It costs around $75 dollars and is a helpful tool to push your career in the right direction of being a powerful woman in the beauty industry. According to the CEW website, "CEW is an international organization of 10,000+ individual members representing a cross section of beauty and related businesses. Members represent leading brands, indies, retailers, media, and suppliers. CEW's purpose is to provide programs that develop careers and knowledge of the beauty industry through industry leader talks, trend reports, newsletters, and mentoring."[13] It's worth looking into, especially if Wende Zomnir, the brains and beauty behind Urban Decay, recommends it.

---

13   "About CEW—Cosmetic Executive Women." 2019. Cosmetic Executive Women. https://www.cew.org/about-cew/.

Wende's story demonstrates that it is okay to push boundaries in makeup. The look you like may seem rogue to some people, but to other people, it's the next big trend in makeup. In addition, she never fails to recognize her team and business partner as catalysts to her success. Wende stresses having a strong business strategy and a close-knit work group, because a quality product will not be enough. Anyone can make a good makeup product. It's who you help and how you strategize that make a lasting impact.

Check out Urban Decay Cosmetics at https://www.urban-decay.com/.

CHAPTER 12:

MARY DILLON— ULTA BEAUTY

———

Even if you claim you know nothing about makeup at all, there's one thing you probably have heard of: Ulta Beauty. Throughout the United States, over one thousand Ulta stores have been established, so the odds of seeing one is high. Soon, Ulta even has plans to expand into Canada. Ulta is a beauty lover's dream, but also their worst nightmare. If you walk into Ulta, you'll most likely walk out with something you most definitely didn't go there for. Ulta has the best of the best makeup brands—both high end and drug store—skin care, hair care, and an in-house beauty salon. If you are one of those people who claim you don't know anything about makeup and beauty, Ulta employees will guide you in the right direction with honest suggestions. No, they don't make commission off what you buy. Some of the best products I purchased from Ulta were due to an employee's feedback. Since Ulta is one of my favorite stores of all time—and I know I'm not alone—I thought I'd get to know its CEO, Mary Dillon, who is a star makeupreneur.

Mary Dillon was interviewed by *Fortune* to get a better glimpse of how she was able to turn Ulta into a beauty powerhouse.[14] After all, she is a female CEO of a Fortune 500 company who was ranked above Jeff Bezos of Amazon and Jamie Dimon of J.P. Morgan according to *Fortune's* "2018 Businesspeople of the Year." Fortune 500 companies only have twenty-four female CEOs, and she is one of them. Mary came from humble beginnings that many of us can relate to. Everything she wanted was not handed to her as she grew up as a daughter of a steelworker on the south side of Chicago. She had to work many jobs to pay her way through college at the University of Illinois at Chicago, receiving a degree in marketing.

Being a CEO is something Mary would have never imagined for herself. Growing up, she didn't know anybody in a prominent business role. Before she made it to Ulta, she worked for the Quaker Oats division of PepsiCo, McDonald's Corporate, and, most recently before Ulta, US Cellular. Mary explains, "What I tell people is, it doesn't necessarily matter where you went to school or exactly what you majored in or your background for sure; if you're somebody who shows up and is curious and delivers, and is good to people, and if you're ambitious, this is what I say to women: if you're ambitious embrace that. There's nothing wrong with that. You know, too often I think women are told not to express that, but if that's what you want, I think anything is possible. It's as simple as that." Mary may have not had the cookie cutter background for a CEO of a makeup company, but she had

---

14 Gharib, Susie. 2019. "Ulta CEO Says of Her Success: 'Anything Is Possible' With Hard Work." Fortune. https://fortune.com/2019/01/15/ulta-beauty-ceo-mary-dillon-leadership/.

the right mind-set to get her there. Not only did she take on the role of CEO, but since she has started, she has also grown annual revenues by 22 percent, according to *Fortune*. Her past business experience before Ulta gave her the confidence to lead Ulta Beauty to success. Kim Kardashian-West's makeup line KKW BEAUTY entered Ulta stores in October 2019, and Kylie Jenner's makeup line Kylie Cosmetics entered the stores a year earlier in November 2018. Whether you like them or not, having Kim Kardashian-West's and Kylie Jenner's products in stores is a huge win for Mary Dillion.

Mary Dillon's business savviness comes from thirty years of hard work. She thinks two things really helped her out in the long run. First, she said really caring about what Ulta associates tell her and her business partners regarding what's working and what's not working for them. Second, she really focuses on what the customer wants. Mary said, "Those pieces have really helped me throughout my career to build businesses, and in the case of Ulta Beauty, to build it in a way that's working and growing. And so I think persistence, hard work, ambition, combined with a really keen focus on what drives the business." Listening to other's opinions allows Mary to meet the needs of both her employees and the customers, which makes everyone happy.

Another facet of Mary's success is embracing diversity and inclusion. Since she became the CEO in 2013, Ulta's executive board is now 50 percent women. She said, "Well, you know obviously, we're a business that is really focused on women, not only exclusively, but the majority of our guests are women. And our store associates, for sure, having women in senior positions is important for every business, not just for our business. Having people with different kinds of experience in industries, different ethnicities, and different life experiences are really important for all businesses, and so for us, it only made sense that we needed to start with having more women in senior positions, and I think that's just the beginning."

Ulta has created many opportunities for women of all backgrounds, but Mary does not discount men wanting to join the Ulta community. I have met men working at Ulta stores suggesting the right makeup for me. They were helpful and knew what they were talking, and that's all that matters. Mary said, "I want to make sure men feel they can be successful at our company as well, because it's not only about women. It's not that simple, but I think having people around the table with various points of view who can also collaborate with each other is actually what I think is most important." Mary's efforts to increase diversity have paid off.

Working for a large corporation, you don't ever expect to have contact with the executive staff. But Mary has made a point of traveling to her Ulta stores throughout the United States. She explained, "I'm there to meet our managers and learn about their career paths, aspirations, where they're coming from, where they want to go, and importantly what's working and not working. In any given day in retail, there's things that are working and not working. I can tell you that much. And so I take the themes and learnings in my team, and I make sure that we make changes based on some of those things." Mary is a great example of a CEO who actually cares about her team. She wants to help them grow and have them contribute to the store's success story.

Mary received advice from her friend who worked for her, and that is knowing when you are doing enough. She said, "Just be yourself. Lead with your strengths. Lead with your own voice. Don't feel like you have to do everything everybody wants, but know what the most important things are. So when 80 percent is enough, move on." Mary went above and beyond in her career, and she still does, but she had to accept that not everything is going to be perfect.

From Mary's story, we see humble beginnings that transformed into a beauty empire. Mary remains herself in everything she does. She is not afraid to ask her employees how they feel. She welcomes diversity. She gets to know the human behind each manager at her stores. In a way, she uses the best of her Midwestern values that have positively impacted her success.

To find an Ulta near you, check out this link: https://www.ulta.com/.

CHAPTER 13:

JACKIE AINA—MAKEUP AND DIVERSITY

———

Increasing the diversity in the makeup industry has been a slow process, but in present times, some real change is finally visible. We see makeupreneurs who are women of color and makeup brands offering a wider variety of foundation pigments. As a white woman, I never struggled to see faces like mine being featured in makeup advertisements, nor have I ever struggled to find a perfect shade of foundation or concealer for my skin. For generations, the makeup industry has disregarded a huge chunk of the world's population by not giving people of color someone to relate to and not providing a product that works for their skin tone.

Presently in the United States, nothing is stopping women from being self-starters, and it's amazing. The more diverse faces we see being portrayed in the makeup industry, the more others will feel comfortable in pursuing business opportunities, too. A few years back, I came across Jackie Aina, a black YouTuber who does makeup reviews and tutorials. But really, she does so much more than that. With 1.2 million followers on Instagram and over 3 million subscribers on YouTube, she has a fan base that keeps coming back for more makeup and beauty content, as well as honest conversations about social issues. To find out more about her entrepreneurial journey, I looked into an interview she did for *Fashionista*.[15]

When Jackie Aina started recording herself on YouTube for makeup tutorials, hauls, and reviews, there was still a lack of diversity in the mainstream media, including makeupreneurs. Her following was much smaller back when she started, but her makeup skills were strong and her voice was even stronger. She needed to make black women the center of the conversation since nobody was already doing so. Jackie was a black woman in the makeup industry with not much to work with regarding makeup for her skin tone and very few other makeupreneurs to turn to who looked like her.

Jackie's path into makeupreneurship was definitely not a linear one. When she was in her early twenties, around the same age I am now, Jackie was living a unique life. She was in the military, married, and living in Hawaii. It may have seemed like her life was put together, but she wasn't genuinely happy. In her spare time, she would delve into what was becoming a very popular website at the time and very much so still today: YouTube. She loved watching YouTube videos but really had no drive to create her own. Jackie was known for her makeup looks. She said, "I was always known

---

15   Houlis, Annamarie. 2018. "How Jackie Aina Went From Army Reservist to Beauty Influencer Phenomenon and Activist." Fashionista. https://fashionista.com/2018/06/jackie-aina-makeup-youtube.

as the girl who always had all these colored eye shadows and for doing all these really bold looks with my dark skin." Her friend convinced her to start a YouTube channel to share her personality and makeup looks with the world. Jackie claims her "number-one true love" was fashion and beauty, so she gave in and started a channel.

When Jackie was starting out on YouTube, she realized the only women she saw promoting makeup were white and Asian women. Now that she was on YouTube, she was going to use it as an opportunity to take the popular videos of makeup tutorials and make them applicable for black women. She took charge of the situation and asked makeup counters to help her get the right tools to recreate makeup looks. Jackie explained, "I got tired of feeling rejected, so I learned how to do these things myself instead of counting on someone else to teach me or show me how it works with my complexion. And I was doing it on YouTube, not realizing that I was filling the void not only for myself, but for other people." Without knowing, Jackie was becoming the face of makeup for the black community.

At the time, Jackie was also exploring taboo topics about race and the makeup industry no one else was addressing. Society needed someone like Jackie Aina, someone who was brave enough to point out disparities in the beauty industry. Jackie lit the torch for other black people to have fun with makeup but also to call out problems when they saw them. Even when makeup brands had colors supposedly meant for black skin, they really weren't. The colors were off, even appearing gray-ish on the skin. One single dark shade of foundation does not cover the many different shades among women of color.

Basically, if you were extremely lucky, the one dark shade available would work for you. But probably not.

Jackie assumed her YouTube channel wasn't going to grow like the rest of the beauty vloggers because they were not addressing these tough topics like she was. But she was okay with it, because she was speaking her truth. During this time, she never even thought she could become a businesswoman out of the YouTube experience. She had no idea she could make money from advertisements and strike deals with makeup companies. Today, the makeup industry is changing for the better, but the change wouldn't have been possible without Jackie Aina or the other black influencers. It's been a topic for years, but real progress has only been made over the last couple of years.

Even though Jackie spends a lot of time advocating for black women, she wants to make it clear that her audience is diverse, and she welcomes everyone. Jackie said, "Now, I don't just have black women that follow me. I don't even have just women that follow me; I have men that follow me, I have nonbinary people that follow me, I have Asian people that follow me, I have white people that follow me, I have Latin people that follow me. So, I always do my best to say that, if you come to my channel, you don't have to necessarily relate to what I'm going through, but I want you to understand and I also want you to learn something. I don't want it to just be about putting on foundation and lipstick, or what the newest launch is. I want people to walk away feeling like they learned something." Even if you can't relate to being a black woman struggling to fit into the beauty industry, it opens up a learning opportunity for those who don't have

102 · MAKEUPRENEUR

this firsthand experience. I am a huge fan of Jackie Aina. Without watching some of her videos, I would have never realized there were major flaws in the beauty industry.

Jackie is not only an advocate, but also highly skilled at the craft of makeup. In addition, she is fun, knowledgeable, and down to earth, which makes for a likable YouTube star. She's got me subscribed. Jackie wanted to be the first dark-skinned female YouTuber to hit one million subscribers, and she did it, and then tripled her subscribers from there! Even though Jackie's makeup choices work the best for darker skin tones, she has all kinds of useful tips, tricks, and reviews for all makeup lovers of all skin tones. Now she enjoys being her true goofy self on camera, but in the beginning, it was tough for her to let loose. She describes herself constantly being in "teach mode" because of her background of being the oldest of seven siblings, the military, and her makeup artistry. When she decided to be herself, her popularity skyrocketed. She's a self-starter, and even today she comes up with her own video ideas that she does weekly. Her success is solely due to her own ambition and drive. From the idea to the production to the editing, she does it all.

Jackie even caught the attention of Too Faced Cosmetics, a favorite of many. The brand collaborated with her to make its foundation shades more inclusive. This a big step for a large company like Too Faced, but it is well overdue. In addition, she has worked with Anastasia Beverly Hills to include highly pigmented eyeshadow shades that would complement women with dark skin tones. Her makeup knowledge paired with her strong voice allows her to be a credible source for the beauty community. In 2018, the National Association for the Advancement of Colored People (NAACP) awarded Jackie with its YouTuber of The Year award. According to its official website, "The mission of the National Association for the Advancement of Colored People (NAACP) is to secure the political, educational, social, and economic equality of rights in order to eliminate race-based discrimination and ensure the health and well-being of all persons." Among its many programs, the organization awards outstanding performances by people of color in film, television, music, and literature.[16]

In addition, Jackie was recognized as a United Nations Change Ambassador. YouTube and the United Nations collaborated to hire female creators from around the world to answer the question, "How can we raise awareness about differences and worldly issues?"

From the Too Faced foundation collaboration to the NAACP award to the recognition from the United Nations, Aina's work has been paying off extensively. Jackie Aina shows us how powerful it can be to be an entrepreneur while tying makeup and social change together. What being a makeupreneur looks like does not come with a handbook, and Jackie shows us a very unique angle the world needs.

Check out Jackie's YouTube channel at https://www.youtube.com/user/lilpumpkinpie05.

---

16   "NAACP | About-Us." 2019. NAACP. https://www.naacp.org/.

CHAPTER 14:

GREGG RENFREW— BEAUTYCOUNTER

―――

Beautycounter has been frequently popping up on my phone while I'm scrolling through social media. Some of these advertisements are coming from people I know, one being a high school friend of mine who is a consultant for the brand. I thought this was a perfect opportunity to explore the new makeup line. Although I hadn't heard about Beautycounter previously, the line was created in 2013 by Gregg Renfrew. Gregg Renfrew is a well-established and powerful business-woman. So, once again, I listened to a podcast on ABC radio in which Rebecca Jarvis interviewed Gregg Renfrew. I highly recommend "No Limits with Rebecca Jarvis." She interviews successful businesswomen from all walks of life, and she gets the best stories and advice for her listeners.[17] It is empower-ing to hear about all these prosperous female entrepreneurs, especially if you have hopes of being a self-starter one day.

―――――――――

17   ABC. 2017. "#23: Gregg Renfrew, Beautycounter Founder and CEO." Podcast. No Limits With Rebecca Jarvis.

Gregg knew from an early age in life that she was meant to do big things. She firmly believes that if you are good at something, you should put all of your energy into it, so you can push yourself forward with poise. That does not mean you have to have all the answers on day one. Gregg didn't even have a business degree, and that turned out perfectly okay. She was an English major in college because she knew being able to communicate to people was just as important as, or even more important than, what you learn in business school. Gregg told Rebecca, "I always say to people, 'You know, I don't care what business you're in — you're in the people business. And if you can communicate properly, with people both orally and written, however we want to do it, that will really help you in business. And I think strong communication is at the core." As a communication major, I see how the degree can allow you to adapt to a vast variety of fields. People may think an English or a communication degree is pointless, but I wholeheartedly disagree. If you are not a competent communicator in the world of business, you will never accomplish your goals. I've spoken to doctors who wish they received more communication training in medical school. Something as simple as being able to communicate well with others can get you farther than a degree ever will. Being able to communicate has allowed Gregg Renfrew to pave her way in the beauty market, as well as in her other successful business endeavors.

Behind the rising success of Beautycounter are Gregg's consistent messages about what sets Beautycounter apart from the rest of the competition, which is their clean ingredients. Customers truly want to hear your authentic story, and Gregg feeds off of that. Gregg claims she's powered her business through storytelling. Beautycounter works by using independent consultants to sell the products, so they are able to tell their personal stories regarding skin care and makeup before and after they found Beautycounter. These beauty consultants get paid by the sales they make, but the corporate angle of Beautycounter handles all of the manufacturing and behind the scenes work that is less glamorous. It's a great business opportunity, according to Gregg, because you get what you put into it. Depending on the hours of work you put into selling the products, some consultants make from $50 a month to $1 million a year. Beautycounter gives an opportunity to people who want to do consult full time, part time, or even sporadically. This works for college students who want some extra "going out" money, hard workers who are struggling to make ends meet, a bored stay-at-home mom, or even a single dad trying to support his children. No guidelines have been created. Some people may not like the idea of direct sales, but Gregg has made it clear that it's a great opportunity for people interested in beauty sales, and it has positively impacted her business. Beautycounter has around twenty thousand people from the United States and Canada selling their products.

Not only are Beautycounter and its consultants financially successful, but also the company's intentions are pure. First, Gregg felt like she needed to educate consumers on what is really going on with the products they are using. Gregg said, "I felt a need to educate people on the need for safer ingredients and the products that they use every day. Once I learned that we were being exposed to toxic chemicals through a variety of means, I wanted people to better understand, so that they could make smart choices for themselves and their families." Second, Gregg wanted to find a solution by creating safe, yet effective beauty products, which is what you get today when you purchase Beautycounter products. Third, the brand is big on advocating for health protective laws. Beautycounter is looking at the bigger picture, which is banning harmful toxins and chemicals in all beauty products. As mind-boggling as it is, Gregg points out that no beauty regulations have been updated since 1938. That's before World War II officially ended. It's been around eighty years since the government has showed any real concern for the beauty industry. Many makeup companies take advantage of the cheap ingredients that are not regulated by the government. Eighty thousand chemicals have been introduced to makeup and skin care brands since the last regulation. Less than 10 percent have been proven safe for humans. Around ten thousand chemicals are commonly used in beauty and cosmetic products, so when Beautycounter started in 2013, the team wanted to make sure to start off on a cleaner path. Beautycounter vowed to make sure 1,500 ingredients will never be used in any of its products to ensure cleaner and healthier cosmetics.

Before Gregg created Beautycounter, she worked in retail entrepreneurship. She was familiar with running a business, but not something as big as Beautycounter. To get where she is now in the makeup industry, she said, "I surrounded myself by with people who are, you know, smarter than I am, but also had expertise in areas that I didn't. So, I don't come from the media industry. I had no business background whatsoever." Of course, Gregg is smart to begin with, but she decided to partner up with Lucy Coleman, a celebrity makeup artist. Lucy would be able to support Gregg's venture into the makeup industry with her solid knowledge about the makeup industry. In addition, she connected with Gina Murphy, someone who had experience with direct sales and could help Beautycounter build its consultant program. In short, Gregg had to find herself business partners that would care just as much about the safety of their beauty products but would also care about the effectiveness and creativeness.

All the new and potential makeupreneurs out there should look to other makeup businesses to see where they went wrong. Gregg takes ownership of all of the little mistakes that were made in the early stages of creating Beautycounter. Beautycounter was not Gregg's first entrepreneurial experience, but it was her first experience in the makeup industry. For starters, she said, "As an entrepreneur, sometimes it's nice to surround yourself with people who you can talk with and support you. But they aren't necessarily the right people for the specific jobs that, you know, are tasks at hand." If you don't set proper guidelines for your friends who are your business partners, you can lose not only the professional relationship, but also the friendship. Of course, friends and family have worked out fine for various makeupreneurs who I mention in this book, such as Huda Beauty, Laura Mercier, and Shelly Maguire who all have family business partners. It all depends on what works best for you. Gregg also admits that she should have looked into better technological resources for her company. Having the latest and greatest technology that fits your company's needs can only benefit you. Gregg says because they did not immediately have the right technology for her unique company, they are still playing catch up. Beautycounter does not use a traditional e-commerce platform because customers are buying from various consultants across the United States and Canada, so each consultant needs their own sales code and commission sales apart from the money that goes directly to Beautycounter. This takes me back to Wende Zomnir from Urban Decay, who stresses how vital it is to have a strong business structure. Gregg quickly fixed her mistake and invested in better technology for her company, which is a large aspect of Beautycounter's structure.

Independent beauty consultants are largely to thank for the success of Beautycounter. Not to say Beautycounter is the most well-known brand out there, but it has been making strides in the beauty industry because of its transparency. The beauty consultants act as educators for the many customers who don't know anything involving the safety of makeup. In turn, they are providing an example of a safer alternative, which is Beautycounter. They are also giving other people the opportunity to join the Beautycounter team so they can make their own business out of the experience whether that be full time or for some extra cash. Since I have a personal connection to the brand, I decided to reach out to my friend Riley, who is an independent consultant for Beautycounter. Riley loves Beautycounter for a few reasons. She said, "First, they truly do abide by their mission statement. Bringing safer products into the hands of customers can be a tough gig, but I feel like they are constantly sharing new info with consultants and clients on how they're doing so. They do a good job of explaining specific ways that their products are safer for our skin as well as the environment. Second, they're working really hard to bring positive reform to the beauty industry across the US. The executive team as well as consultants from all over have been lobbying in Washington to increase regulations on chemicals used in products, with positive results! Multiple new laws have been passed in California and Hawaii about reducing chemical use in beauty and sun screen products. Baby steps, but I think they're doing an amazing job of working towards the long-term goal of a federal bill being passed."

I admire the brand's openness. The executives are honest and knowledgeable about what exactly is in their products. With most companies, the consumer is in the dark. Which ingredients are harmful is not common knowledge. Beautycounter is exposing the beauty industry and working toward making change, and doing it all with poise.

As a for-profit organization, Beautycounter has the ability to move markets quicker than nonprofit organizations. Not that nonprofit organizations don't make an impact, but Gregg thinks if you have an affinity toward a certain brand, you are going to be influenced to join in on their mission. For example, if you are a loyal customer to Nike and Nike is working toward getting laws passed that ban wasteful materials for packaging shoes, you may be inclined to buy from a company that is trying to make environmentally conscious choices while you are getting a Nike purchase out of it. Gregg said, "You should be able to build businesses that are highly profitable, create tons of jobs for people that are simultaneously moving markets and doing things that are good for the world." Building a strong profitable business and doing good for the world do not need to be mutually exclusive. When it comes to using cheaper ingredients that may jeopardize your health versus using ingredients that are far more expensive but health conscious, Beautycounter is going to take the financial risk of utilizing safer ingredients every time. Gregg admitted that "the honest truth is the world does not need another beauty business. What we need is safer products and families to be healthier." There need to be more unique, innovative, and health-conscious products. Slowly but surely, we are seeing a demand for this. Consumers are now looking for makeup companies that are transparent and making choices to benefit the environment and their health. Gregg said, "I think at the end of the day, you have to genuinely authentically want to do it." Don't be the company that sells a hazardous beauty product masked in hot pink packaging to gain sales off a popular campaign such as Susan G. Komen's breast cancer fund. Be the company that makes a natural, chemical-free lipstick that would 100 percent certain never cause cancer. Beautycounter is one of the first companies that is calling it out as it is.

"I would say most entrepreneurs that I know, if they're really an entrepreneur—they have a driving passion inside. They see an issue of an opportunity, and they want to address that with a solution that makes sense for the marketplace," Gregg explained. Time and time again, successful makeupreneurs have brought up the importance of passion. If you can't ignite the fire inside of you, can you really make it as a self-starter? Maybe, but without that passion, you won't really love what you do.

"I feel that I was put on this Earth to do something—I had the ability to do something important in the business world. And I think for me, the opportunity to create a business that was actually going to move a market in the right direction, which would actually lead to a safer and healthier country, is something that I just felt incredibly compelled to do. I know, of course, I want to build a business that is financially successful, and we have been, but to me, it's really about how do you use the time that you have to do something extremely important and to bring people along with you in this journey. And I think it's been the thing that gets me up. I mean, I think I have the greatest job in the world. And I'm so lucky to work with this incredible team of women and men, and to be able to, you know, build this platform upon which people have built businesses and hopefully in time seen more health protective laws in this country. And I think at the end of the day, we're not going to give up until we see that this industry change because it needs to." Now Gregg is an entrepreneur that everyone can look up to, even if makeup is not your passion. She's excited to get to work every day to work with makeup and fight for change.

Gregg Renfrew's story is an honest and passionate one. Her story teaches us how relevant communication is to any career, but especially entrepreneurship. In addition, finding partners who can fill in your knowledge gaps will benefit you tremendously. She's not afraid to admit the many mistakes she made while launching Beautycounter. New makeupreneurs can learn from her mistakes, but also contribute to her fight for cleaner cosmetics.

CHAPTER 15:

LAURA CRONIN—CLEAN-FACED COSMETICS

———

Kool-Aid packets, glitter, petroleum jelly, lanolin: all the products needed to create your own lip gloss. Quite a gross lip gloss if you think about it, and that's exactly how Laura Cronin, creator of Clean-Faced Cosmetics, would describe it. As a junior high student in a lip gloss making class, Laura was taught those are the core ingredients to make lip gloss. Sure, those can work, but they are not vital in creating a quality lip gloss. This reminds me of when I was younger and I would make my own lip gloss for how-to speeches in school. It was quite simple. All I did was take Vaseline, vanilla or mint flavoring, and my eyeshadow of choice for a hint of color. It was fun and crafty, so I understand why Laura got pulled into the world of making homemade makeup. As Laura reached college, it was time for her to move into the eco-friendly, cruelty-free realm of DIY makeup. Money was tight, so after some time of saving up, she was able to buy a handful of materials to work with via trial and error. A couple years later, the college degree that Laura received wasn't getting her where she wanted to be. She found herself at the photo counter at the drug store, which is not exactly how she imagined life after college.

The photo counter job didn't provide much for Laura to work with in terms of money or enjoyment. So Laura started making homemade makeup creations for her friends, family, and coworkers as a way of connecting back to her childhood roots. They would give her honest feedback about her products so improve them. It was more than a hobby. Laura genuinely wanted to be using clean makeup that is better for the environment and doesn't hurt animals in the process. With enough feedback accumulating, Laura knew she could launch her products on Etsy. Etsy is "an e-commerce website focused on handmade or vintage items and supplies, as well as unique factory-manufactured items." If you have a passion for creating your own unique products, Etsy is a great place to start, and Laura had the right product to share with the Etsy community. Clean-Faced Cosmetics is completely vegan and does not test on animals, leaving a great slogan for the company: "Tested on Friends, Not Animals." According to the *New York Times* article "Why You Should Care About Vegan Beauty," common ingredients used in beauty products are honey, beeswax, wool grease, shark liver oil, crushed up beetles, animal bones, ligaments, urine, organs, and whale vomit. If this grossed you out in the slightest, you should probably do your research before you make your next purchase. If you don't want to do the research, Clean-Faced Cosmetics certainly is not using any of the ingredients listed above.

A lot of thought has gone into Clean-Faced Cosmetics. Two of Laura's favorite creations are her volumizing agave mascara and lash-lengthening powder. According to Laura, "Nearly all conventional mascaras rely on silicones and alcohol to dry and stay put, so formulating one with neither of those ingredients was truly a challenge and required months of trial and error. But it was worth it!" Laura is a great example of caring much more about what goes into her products than becoming a money-making machine. Laura Cronin has a similar passion to Gregg Renfrew, creator of Beautycounter: promoting safe makeup. The difference is Laura has started from ground zero and is the one behind every aspect of the business from the actual creating of the makeup to packaging to customer relations. In addition, Laura focuses on being environmentally friendly. A lot of her packaging is reusable and is meant to be sent back and refilled for more product.

Her natural and clean products are hard to pass up when you know that thousands of products out there are using chemicals that are unregulated. As Clean-Faced Cosmetics grows, the hope is to expand to more stockists so the brand reaches more homes. Also, Laura is a one woman show. "Oh gosh, and I need to hire someone," Laura laughed; she fills fifty to seventy orders a week and counting.

What Laura does is definitely not for everyone. Crafting and marketing a homemade product can take all of your effort and time, but that's what being a makeupreneur is. Having a resilient personality type is crucial, and Laura claims that it wasn't always something she had, but something she worked on. If you have a niche for something and have a bold personality, I don't see why you shouldn't take the risk. Nobody said being a real self-starter was easy.

Explore Clean-Faced Cosmetics at https://www.facebook.com/cleanfacedcosmetics/.

CHAPTER 16:

AISHETU DOZIE— BOSSY COSMETICS

Makeup is looked at much differently today than it ever was before. Companies are transforming negative stereotypes into positive ones. People are wearing makeup to empower themselves and others. I wanted to find a brand that embodies the empowerment of women and makeup simultaneously. That is when I came in contact with the ever-so-humble CEO of Bossy Cosmetics, Aishetu Fatima Dozie.

When I first talked to Aishetu Dozie, she was excited and nervous about the upcoming launch of Bossy Cosmetics in March 2019. Launching a cosmetic line is certainly a gamble, and Aishetu had no doubts about that. Aishetu's professional resume is so impressive, however, that it would be hard to believe someone as accomplished as her would be nervous about starting a makeup line. Her educational background consists of Cornell University, Harvard Kennedy School, Stanford University, and the Harvard Business School. She is a sophisticated banker who has worked for Lehman Brothers,

Morgan Stanley, Standard Chartered Bank, and Rand Merchant Bank. Aishetu has done so much beyond banking. She is the founder of African HERstory. According to its website, African HERstory creates "visual content about ambitious and inspirational black women in Africa and the Americas."[18] Aishetu is clearly already successful, but she still had a passion for makeup that she couldn't forget about. It doesn't matter what your profession or background is—if you want to explore a new and exciting business venture, the power is all yours. Since I've spoken to Aishetu, Bossy Cosmetics' official launch date has passed. Bossy Cosmetics currently sells lip products through its website, Amazon, and Facebook.

When I asked her how she got started, Aishetu laughed and said, "Yeah, I'm still starting. I think you never stop starting." Improvements must always be made, and making sure your products are ethical, cruelty-free, and vegan is a challenge in itself. Bossy Cosmetics wants people to feel empowered in the shopping experience. Opportunities to virtually try on lipsticks are available on the website. Makeup consumers know it's a hassle and unsanitary to try on lipsticks in the store, so this most definitely improves the shopping experience. When shopping online, you have no idea if the shade of lipstick you are buying will look good on you. Bossy Cosmetics is bringing a great tool to the table, and other companies can learn from using the best of technology to enhance the shopping experience. In addition, Bossy Cosmetics will also have a blog that will feature successful entrepreneurs around the world. People such as designer Tory Birch, Nigerian supermodel

---

18 "Welcome to African Herstory-Black Girl Magic Lives and Rules Here." 2019. Welcome To African Herstory. https://www.africanherstory.com/.

Mayowa, and Katie Bouman, who gave us the first image of a black hole, are just some of the badass chicks Bossy Cosmetics has featured on its page. It's empowering to see a company that uplifts women of all colors, shapes, and sizes. Better yet, Aishetu knows how to handle money wisely as a banker and knows how to create a spotlight that empowers women from all walks of life through African HERstory. Aishetu's professional expertise matched with utilizing the best of social media and technology will be very important in the success of Bossy Cosmetics.

As a professional working woman, Aishetu chose makeup because she has always struggled with the idea of confidence and how she feels and presents herself. Thoughts such as "Do I have executive presence?" and "How is this room viewing me?" entered her mind. Because of this, Aishetu wants other woman to feel empowered by her makeup. It starts with lipstick. "Some women want a bold lipstick to feel amazing, others want a lipstick to go out and conquer the world," Aishetu said. This message immediately resonated with me, as a pop of color on my lips definitely makes me feel good. "We focus on how women feel over how they look," Aishetu said, which is the guiding line for Bossy Cosmetics. It is important that every woman feels beautiful with makeup or not. This is the type of company I want to support.

Aishetu is looking forward to receiving feedback. She wants to know what customers love and what can be approved. Another aspect that customers can take pride in is donating on the website to multiple nonprofits if you choose to do so. Bossy Cosmetics is aiming to be a beauty line with a purpose. Bossy partners with Women at Risk International

Foundation (WARIF), which is based in Nigeria. In short, "WARIF is a nonprofit organization founded by Dr. Kemi DaSilva-Ibru in response to high incidence of sexual assault, rape, and human trafficking occurring amongst young girls and women across Nigeria." WARIF is meant to spread awareness on the topic of sexual abuse, prevent it from happening, and treat the women affected by the abuse.[19] Buying from Bossy Cosmetics will directly contribute to the cause. The best way to empower women is to help other women, and Bossy Cosmetics is already mastering this concept.

I have seen Bossy Cosmetics grow tremendously in only a few months. The line has already been featured in *Refinery29, Allure, Marie Claire, Essence,* and more. Aishetu's amazing journey shows that if you have a strong message, others will want to join in your movement. This brand is one you will want to look out for, as it is quickly building momentum.

To check out Bossy Cosmetics go to https://bossybeauty.com/.

---

19   "WARIF—Women at Risk International Foundation." 2019. Warifng.Org. https://warifng.org/.

CHAPTER 17:

KAYLEY AND BLAKE MILLER—PAWS BEAUTY

———

When starting your own makeup line, you can really channel anything you like. Don't believe me? I talked to a makeupreneur who was able to create a makeup line revolving around one of her biggest passions in life.

"Beauty with a higher purpose, 100% cruelty-free," is the mission behind this makeupreneur's company. Just like Gregg Renfrew, founder of Beautycounter, and Aishetu Dozie, founder of Bossy Cosmetics, Paws Beauty has a mission behind it. Beautycounter focuses on pushing legislation for safer beauty products. Bossy Cosmetics shines light on women's empowerment, while supporting causes for women. Paws Beauty, of course, focuses on saving the lives of animals. When you are an entrepreneur, specifically a makeupreneur, you have the freedom to come up with a product that is truly meaningful to you. Couple Kayley and Blake Miller are the hearts and brains behind Paws Beauty. Paws Beauty donates 20 percent of its net profit to various shelters and organizations committed to helping animals in need. Helping animals, especially dogs, hits close to home for the Millers, as they have adopted four dogs from various shelters throughout the United States whose names are Toby, Onyx, Sofi, and Pike. In 2019, the nonprofit of choice was Pets Without Parents, which is a no-kill animal shelter dedicated to finding homes for cats and dogs.

When it comes to the actual knowledge of makeup, Kayley Miller has been invested in makeup for years. Kayley was going to give makeup blogging a try to share her best beauty tips and to give out makeup recommendations to the general public until she built a fan base like most makeupreneurs do. As mentioned in Chapter 1, Huda Kattan tirelessly blogged until she met some type of traction. Kayley had plans of going that route, but she had a supportive partner who was willing to take a bigger risk with her. Go big or go home was the way Kayley's husband thought. They sought out a manufacturer to get Kayley's eyeshadow visions made. It took them about four months to get a perfect metallic eyeshadow formula and then about eight months to get a matte eyeshadow formula they were happy with. They have been selling their metallic eyeshadows since February 2019 their matte formula since July 2019. To stay afloat in the beauty industry, the Millers pride themselves in giving the customers exactly what they want. Customers wanted a magnetic eyeshadow palette design, so they released one. Customers asked for a matte eyeshadow palette, so the Millers made that happen, too. The Millers are on a mission to make a difference by promoting cruelty-free products and helping shelters through donations. They want to make sure their products are profitable for the animals' sake, but also because real makeup lovers like what they are putting out in the market. It's all about giving the customer what they want while still being able to support a positive end goal.

The Millers advised self-starters to start slowly. Kayley said, "If possible, produce only in small amounts of products at a time and order a new batch as you need it. It can be more expensive that way at first because you're buying less in bulk, but the benefit of not having hundreds of shades that's not selling well outweighs the costs." This way you can see which makeup products are actually selling before making an extreme commitment.

Being the best makeupreneur you can be requires passion, and that is seen throughout the various makeupreneurs in this book. The Millers have a passion for animals and makeup, so making that into a collaborative business was the smart move for them. Creating a line that helps others in need will speak to the masses. Their story shows us that when starting a makeup line, you can start out slow and with ease. Find out what works before you invest all of your money at once.

Check out Paws Beauty at https://www.pawsbeautyllc.com/.

CHAPTER 18:

SHILPI JAIN—SKINVEDA

Maybe I should have payed closer attention in chemistry class. Behind the scenes of a makeup company, a chemist in a lab somewhere is using scientific formulas to create a makeup masterpiece. Makeup brands have many facets that you might consider, but one of my most important elements is having someone who can actually develop the product. One of the coolest makeupreneurs I got to talk to was actually a chemist for her own makeup and skin care line.

Shilpi Jain started mixing things together as a child, hoping to spark up unique reactions and formulas. She was destined to become a chemist, but little did she know she would be the brains behind her own beauty company, Skinveda. One master's degree in chemistry later, Shilpi found herself working in the pharmaceutical industry. Eventually, Shilpi and her family moved to Texas, but she quickly found out there was a lack of job opportunities in the field of pharmaceuticals and drug development despite her credentials. Without much of a choice, Shilpi needed to explore other options for herself. She soon found herself working at a cosmetic manufacturing firm, where she started from ground zero. Shilpi loved creating her own unique mixtures as a child, but becoming a cosmetic chemist was something she had little professional experience with other than dabbling in the creation of perfumes at a previous job. Persistently working hard allowed for upward movement in the company as well as a thirst for knowledge. Shilpi explained, "It really helped me integrate my chemistry knowledge and knowledge of pharmaceuticals, because to develop a formula it's not just about kitchen chemistry where you just mix up things." More specifically, she really wanted to focus on the knowledge of human skin and the delivery system in creating a formula that enriches the skin. She did not want to look back, especially after she had the opportunity to work on several celebrity cosmetic lines. Shilpi liked what she was doing, and she was only moving forward in the cosmetic industry.

Shilpi Jain is certainly a career-oriented woman, but she is a dedicated mother as well. Shilpi's son had acute eczema. As she became well acquainted with the chemistry and formulation of products now that she worked in a cosmetics lab, she was well aware that skin care products can be ironically harsh. Many include harmful ingredient that are directly absorbed into the skin. A lot of well-known companies are not transparent when it comes to their ingredients, which is highly concerning. This was a perfect opportunity for Shilpi to formulate a replenishing serum to help with her son's condition. Without any formal plans, she was soon going to become a self-starter. With her being the lead on this project, she would never consider putting harmful ingredients in it, even if it was the cheaper option. Shilpi said, "Safety was very important, because a lot of companies are not basing their products on protecting the consumer but more focused on fragrance, packaging, and the cheapest possible ingredients." This was no easy process, but with a mother's simultaneous passion for her child and her career, Shilpi went on for a few years to create something natural and highly effective for her beloved son.

Word of mouth has a larger impact than one might expect in the rise of a company. The replenishing serum was successful for her son, so Shilpi wasn't shy to share how her 100 percent natural creation worked for her son. Shilpi's OBGYN was interested in trying out this serum for her patients with rosacea because of the natural and effective ingredients. One thing led to the next, and acquaintances of Shilpi were requesting more original creations, such as cellulite cream. In the process, she gained loyal customers. So she quit her job and put all of her energy into creating products that are natural. Today she creates and sells BB creams, toners, cleansers, moisturizers, and various oils. You can even take a quiz that will direct you to the best products for your skin. Shilpi genuinely cares about the ingredients she puts in her products and intends for it to improve the mind, body, and soul, reaching into Indian teachings she lives by. For now, Shilpi is the main chemist of her small, self-made company, but it is certainly growing as beauty consumers are becoming more conscious of what they are putting on and around their bodies. She hires part-time technicians and packagers, and as her company grows, so will the number of employees she needs to hire. Local stores and salons who are on the same mission as Shilpi are frequent distributors of her products.

As unique as Shilpi's story is, she believes anyone who has the right drive can create their own beauty line. Consulting is another one of Shilpi's roles, as she can help people from varied backgrounds create a beauty line for themselves. Although she believes having a chemistry background was critical in her own career, she also believes anyone can do this with dedication, experience, and lifelong learning. She said, "Many people who come into this industry have varied backgrounds. It can be someone who is an interior designer or someone who just loves looking after their skin, and then they decide they want to make this happen." She actually highly recommends people getting into the field, especially as chemists and technicians. It really helps, but she said you don't necessarily need a chemistry degree either. It just helps you understand important aspects of chemicals and how they react with the skin.

Shilpi was not automatically a businesswoman. It was a work in progress, as it will be for anyone trying to make a name for themselves in the beauty industry, especially working with natural products. Shilpi is in the social media game, and claims if her company was not participating in social media, just being an entrepreneur is not enough to make it. No matter what roadblocks come up while working strictly with natural products and making a name for oneself, Shilpi wouldn't have it any other way.

It was refreshing to hear someone talk about how much they care about the health of their customers, rather than using cheap ingredients in expense of our safety. Her story shows us that if you have a passion for learning, you too can be the brains behind the actual formulations of a beauty brand.

With the knowledge of chemicals put into our makeup products, you will have power to create ethical makeup and skin care for consumers.

To see more about Skinveda check out https://www.skinveda.com/.

CHAPTER 19:

GINAMARIE MCGUIRE— GINAMARIE

———

Inheriting the family business can be the best thing that happens to you or the worst thing. Working in the makeup industry was Gina Marie McGuire's mother's passion, even naming her company GINAMARIE in tribute to her daughter. In Gina's case of inheriting the family business, it turned out to be a great thing.

At first, Gina wanted to stray from the family business and become a teacher. But eventually she realized the significance of the skin care and makeup industry in her life. Gina explained that she realized, "Being a teacher does not restrict you to the walls of a school classroom." Teachers are necessary but currently lacking in the beauty industry. And I don't mean makeup artist instructors—I mean someone credible who teaches consumers about what is in their products and how to maintain healthy skin. Gina knew her heart was still in the family company because she was able to teach others. She created a satellite company of GINAMARIE, originally in Florida, in a Chicago suburb in hopes to carry on the family name.

Today, Gina is working hard at GINAMARIE, following in her mother's footsteps. Gina said, "I am teaching others what true beauty is." Gina teaches classes for people such as estheticians who specialize in giving skin treatments and waxes, including classes for children. If you are still trying to discover what true beauty is, maybe a class with Gina is what you need. Hint: true beauty does not involve wearing a lot of makeup. Gina also has an internship program for students who want to learn how to use social media to run a business and educate others on skin health.

Gina takes pride in teaching people about their skin while promoting confidence. Becoming a teacher was something Gina always wanted to do, and in her own unique way she is teaching people every day. Forty years strong with many loyal customers, the family business must be doing something right.

I respect the mission behind GINAMARIE. Makeup companies seldom teach us about our skin as an organ and what products are safe to use. Gina's business shows us that having a family member in the makeup industry may inspire you to follow in their footsteps while creating your own unique twist. She also shows us that being a teacher is another role of a makeupreneur.

To find out more check out https://ginamarieproducts.com/.

CHAPTER 20:

SHELLY MAGUIRE

———

Somedays we don't feel pretty. Somedays we may not feel good about ourselves. But when someone is dealing with a medical disease or ailment, these bad days may appear too often. I came across someone who made a career out of coming up with a product to make you feel better on your worst days. Her name is Shelly Maguire.

Talking to Shelly Maguire put a smile on my face. She is a confident and amiable lady, so it is no surprise that she has made a name for herself in the beauty industry. Beauty and health have always caught Shelly's attention because of some of the health challenges she has faced throughout her life. She has cystic fibrosis and admits that she wasn't really happy with the way she looked or felt. Sometimes, you have to take charge of the way you look and feel, and Shelly took advantage of all the opportunities life gave her.

One day, Shelly was sitting in her hair salon and overheard the owner saying she would get rid of her salon if someone just took care of payments. This peaked Shelly's interest, so she approached the owner and made a deal, not knowing anything about the ins and outs of the business. She had a vision of what she wanted: everything health, wellness, and beauty related—a one-stop shop, to be exact. Shelly said, "It was a stop where you can get everything you need. It was like an Ulta or Sephora before an Ulta or Sephora even existed." I guess you could say Shelly was ahead of the times.

Shelly tells people to always "look for opportunity everywhere. Always be listening. Keep your eyes and ears open. Because something might pass you, and if you don't take advantage of the situation, you change your life for the worse or the better." And that's exactly how Shelly primarily got started in the beauty business, by taking that opportunity one day while sitting in her local beauty salon. Just being open to new people and experiences can transform your career.

A product Shelly created that really got her name on the map was her two-minute miracle gel, a seven-in-one product for the face. The product serves as a cleanser, toner, exfoliator, hydrator, brightener, pore minimizer, and primer for the skin, all while using powerful natural ingredients like collagen boosting peptides, wrinkle removing proteins, and antioxidants from moringa oleifera—a type of tree—and mango seeds. The product gained popularity as Shelly sold it through salons and made appearances at trade shows and home parties. She wanted to create something that would be effective and simple all packed into one product, because she knows how confusing and expensive skin care gets. Shelly also knew what it felt like to not feel good about one's appearance, so she wanted to give others the opportunity to feel good about themselves.

With her first product's success, she was able to move forward and keep creating. She sold on the Home Shopping Network live for ten years with Guthy-Renker, the direct marketing company. From there, the products she worked on were never ending. Right now, she is making products for three different brands and consulting for other beauty entrepreneurs. For example, she developed Jenni Farley from *Jersey Shore*'s new skin care line, Naturally Woww. You may best know her as JWoww.

Shelly extensively researches ingredients, goes to trade shows, and meets suppliers. Shelly has requirements for all her products: "One, they must be clinically proven, and two, they must be natural." When she finds the right ingredients to form a product, she then brainstorms branding stories that will be intriguing to people.

She is proud of all that she has accomplished. She started from the ground up with no help, and now she is eighteen years strong, working in the forefront of the skin care industry with her husband, who is also her business partner. For all the aspiring beauty entrepreneurs out there, Shelly has some advice to give. She said, "Take something until it doesn't make sense. People run into luck every day, so you have to create your own. You have to have your ears open for opportunity." An opportunity may quickly pass you by, and the key is to be ready to jump on the next one. If you aspire to build a name for yourself in the beauty industry, the answer may be around the corner.

Shelly's story shows us that you need to create your own opportunities. You can't expect success to be handed to you.

She also shows us that the boundaries of being a self-starter in the beauty industry are permeable. She started out by buying a beauty salon and making it a one-stop beauty shop. In addition, consulting for other makeupreneurs is another pathway to success in the beauty industry.

Find out more about Shelly at https://www.facebook.com/ShellyMaguireLive/.

CHAPTER 21:

VANESSA AMAYA— KREIDA COSMETICS

———

Some of the most successful people in life are the ones who have been through the most. Vanessa Amaya is one hell of a women who is in the midst of growing her beauty line, Kreida Cosmetics. Her love for glamorous hair and makeup has always been a huge part of her life, though not always her first priority. Vanessa is a hard-working and loving mother who prioritizes her family above all else. She works long, draining, 40-hour weeks in the medical field and still comes home as a devoted mother and wife.

Vanessa's life certainly hasn't been easy, but that was never an excuse when it came to being a makeupreneur. One of the worst things a mother can hear is finding out her child is sick. In Vanessa's case, her world was turned upside down when her son was diagnosed with brain cancer. With this devastating news, Vanessa truly lost a sense of herself. To escape this funk, Vanessa knew it was time to do something unexpected during this painful time. This unexpected thing was get involved in the makeup business and get her makeup ideas created like she had always longed to do. She needed to do extensive research to find the right manufacturers for her vision. She also required that the makeup be made in U.S., cruelty-free, vegan, and paraben-free.

Everything Kreida Cosmetics launches has a meaningful message behind it. To begin, Vanessa chose the colors of her company to be black and gold, representing childhood Cancer awareness. Vanessa said, "It's a way of giving back to the tight-knit community that helped me so much during the roughest of times with my son." She wants to empower women and inspire mothers that a light at the end of the tunnel does exist. With every sale, she will be donating a portion to Phoenix Children's Cancer Center.

In addition to the connection to the childhood cancer community, the names of her products are Latin-infused, paying homage to her culture. The word "kreida" is a slang word commonly used by the Latin community. It is used to describe someone who is full of themselves. Some of her lipstick names include: Chula, Chiquita, Atrevida, and Susia. In English, the names mean hot, cute/little girl, daring, and dirty. It's all about feeling like a badass and having fun no matter who you are. She was reminiscing on the days that she was young and wild when coming up with the fun names of her products.

The next steps are to create a Kreida collection dedicated to childhood cancer, with a possible name being "hope," but the process is still in the works. Ideally, the line would be sold in the Phoenix Children's Cancer Center gift shop and all proceeds would go to the hospital. Vanessa hopes that the Phoenix Children's Cancer Center can help other children like they helped her family.

It's all about making a difference. Vanessa took everything she had, financially and mentally, to live out her passion. She puts herself out there every day, not for money, but to make a difference. Everyone has a different goal when it comes to being a makeupreneur, and in this case, it is for Vanessa's family and the childhood cancer community.

To see Kreida Cosmetics for yourself go check out https://www.kreidacosmetics.com/.

CHAPTER 22:

CHANTAL DE GREEF— BASIC BEAUTY TOOLS

———

Being a self-starter in the makeup industry does not always mean you need to be creating actual makeup like foundation, lipstick, mascara, and so on. In Chantal De Greef's case, she has made a name for herself creating makeup sponges, sponge cleansers, and drying racks under her company name: Basic Beauty Tools. All of these products are tools that makeup users heavily rely on.

Her story starts from being raised in a humble entrepreneurial family in the United Kingdom. Her dad was an agricultural business owner of silverskin onions. Once Chantal hit fifteen, she was already in work mode. She started working for her dad's business. Then, during college, Chantal started working at a Dior beauty counter, where she believes her interest for the makeup industry was sparked. Her college degree led her down a path of becoming a lawyer, but that did not mean she disregarded her interest in makeup.

What initially got Chantal started in the makeup industry was pure frustration. Frustration regarding expensive beauty tools that were not worth the money. Chantal explained, "I started Spongedry because I was fed up with paying too much for products that were awful. I just got frustrated with the Beauty Blenders bling ring, which you pay around £20 for and when you receive the product, it just looks tacky and does not do a proper job." In US dollars today, that would be around $22.00. That's a lot of money to waste on a product you had high hopes for. Chantal specifically mentioned the Beauty Blender bling ring. The bling ring was made to act as a stand for your beauty blender or makeup sponge to dry. I just googled it, and I'm not going to lie—it's not cute. In her case, the drying rack didn't do its job by holding up the sponge. While damp, it doesn't hold well, and the appearance was cheap looking.

Chantal did not want to put up with all of the disappointments she was facing with makeup tools, so she took matters into her own hands. Having proper makeup tools was actually quite serious for Chantal. She needs things to be clean and tidy, specifically for her rare skin condition. One of the biggest concerns for Chantal is keeping her beauty tools clean to avoid harmful bacteria on her skin. Chantal has Hailey-Hailey skin disease. People with this condition have to be very aware of keeping the skin bacteria-free, as bacteria can cause flare-ups and infections. Hailey-Hailey is a rare disease that needs special care, especially when applying makeup. This gap in the makeup industry fueled the idea behind the creation of Spongedry. Spongedry allows a sponge, wet or dry, to use the stand and avoid harmful bacteria for the skin. Chantal was able to create a brand, Basic Beauty Tools, to meet her needs, as well as the needs of others who may have the same concerns. I have struggled with acne throughout my life, so keeping my beauty tools clean is always a precaution I can take to prevent breakouts. Even if you have clear skin, you should keep your makeup tools clean. You never know what may be lurking on that makeup brush of yours.

Basic Beauty Tools may be innovative, but competing with other beauty tool brands is still a constant challenge. Off the top of my head, I can think of Real Techniques and Eco-Tools, which have been dominating the makeup tool market for years. Chantal explains that "what we see is that big retailers have invested in the leading brands in this field, and they have an established relation with those brands and they are a bit reluctant to take on new products and brands." It is difficult to outshine larger companies that already have a name in the industry; however, Basic Beauty Tools can deliver a high-quality product at an affordable price. She also explained that it can be difficult to find the correct buyers for the retailers you want. Although Chantal has struggled, her company has been featured in various magazines such as *Glamour* and *Traveler,* has been a seller on QVC, and is featured by popular YouTubers.

The next step for Basic Beauty Tools is getting more traction and sales from the company website. With that being said, they still need to enlist an SEO to help. In addition, they are in the process of improving the packaging and making it more environmentally friendly. This includes bringing their packaging down to two elements instead of what they are currently using, which is five elements. Chantal also plans to work with a packaging manufacturer to ensure all packaging is made from recyclable plastic. Basic Beauty Tools also has new product ideas lined up that will depend on having enough resources to make that investment.

What I loved about my conversation with Chantal was her pure honesty. When it comes to just anybody becoming an entrepreneur in the beauty industry, Chantal explained, "I don't know. I think you need a bit of cash or investment to start and then it is still a gamble to see whether the product will take off. If you're prepared to take a gamble (a calculated one of course—you do need to do your research and find out your sales margins and calculate whether you can make money) and are aware of the risk that it can go wrong, then of course everyone could become an entrepreneur. I am not sure that everyone wants to take a gamble, though." Chantal wants people to know how big the risk is, because just like any entrepreneurial venture, it may not always go as planned.

Chantal's story demonstrates how she filled a gap for herself in the beauty industry, because nobody else was. Having a skin disease is extremely tough, but she was able to create a product that would allow her to safely use makeup. She also emphasizes how becoming a self-starter is a risk. So, before moving too quickly, keep in mind the hurdles you will have to face to succeed.

Check out Basic Beauty Tools at https://www.basicbeauty-tools.com/.

CHAPTER 23:

PATRICIA HARTMANN— RUNWAY ROGUE

———

When I think of supermodels, I think of intricate clothing and striking makeup featured in magazines and paraded down runways. Supermodels need to be the best of the best, and so does the makeup on their face.

Patricia Hartmann was a notable '90s supermodel discovered in Germany who is best known for appearing as the face of L'Oréal Paris for many years and covering the front pages of *Vogue, Elle, Marie Claire, Harper's Bazaar, Allure,* and more. This allowed Patricia to build networks with the best names in the makeup industry. Not many people get the opportunity to work with the top names in the beauty industry, so I thought I'd get to know Patricia a little bit better.

Working for L'Oréal Paris allowed Patricia to see the corporate side of the beauty industry, which sparked her passion to create a line of her own. She saw what happened behind the scenes and knew it was something she could do herself. She had the opportunity to get makeup done by various artists such as Kevyn Aucoin, Laura Mercier, Francois Nars, and Bobbi Brown. With the right connections and appropriate experiences, Patricia decided to start her own company called Runway Rogue, giving credit to her exciting career as a supermodel.

Her line focuses on bold lip liners and lipsticks, getting you ready to strut your stuff no matter if you're a supermodel or not. According to *Linger Magazine,* Patricia explains that her beauty line is actually good for you. Many other beauty lines' lip products have drying properties, which is something you don't sign up for when buying the product. Some ingredients Patricia incorporates into her lip products are jojoba oil, aloe vera, and green tea extract. Patricia said, "It's been a hell of an amazing ride, and the company is growing faster than I had ever hoped for." Patricia's life experiences guided her in the right direction to pursue a beauty career from the ground up. Patricia ran the show in the '90s, but now her makeup line is stealing the limelight. Runway Rogue has been used on models during New York Fashion Week 2019, Miami Fashion Week and Miami Swim Week 2019, and LA Fashion Week 2019.

Today, magazines aren't featuring Patricia Hartmann, but they are featuring new and upcoming models wearing her makeup. Runway model Yilena Hernandez was featured on the cover of *Cosmopolitan* magazine wearing Runway Rogue's long wear liquid lipstick, Paparazzi. Patricia's makeup is being used for iconic moments that will bring ultimate exposure to Runway Rogue. Each event is a new opportunity to network and spread the word about her line.

Patricia Hartmann's journey demonstrates how she was able to build upon her glamorous career to make it an even more exciting one with her own makeup launch. Getting a job in the beauty industry whether that be in a corporate role, as a model, or as a photographer for a fashion brand, you are getting experience that can be applied into an entrepreneurial venture.

CHAPTER 24:

DEBRA JENN—THE YOUTUBE PERSONALITY

———

YouTube is the holy grail for finding makeup tutorials and recommendations. Right before I make a new makeup purchase, I will search a review for that specific product. You will get honest feedback and suggestions before you go ahead and spend the money. Makeup can be expensive, so utilizing YouTube is not only smart for your wallet, but also a source of entertainment. People fall in love with YouTubers every day. They are influencers and have an impact on many people. After hitting a certain amount of views and subscribers, you gain credibility and people will trust you, especially if you are good at makeup.

Debra Jenn is an upcoming makeup YouTube star, and I think that makes her a self-starter in the makeup industry. As I said before, being an entrepreneur in the beauty industry comes in all shapes and sizes. It is extremely common for a YouTuber who creates makeup tutorials and reviews beauty products to make a name for themselves in the makeup industry and grow their personal brand. If you have a magnetic personality and useful makeup knowledge, YouTube channels are a powerful tool.

Like most successful and honest makeupreneurs, their journey is ignited with a simple passion for makeup. Debra herself loved watching tutorials of beauty gurus. She tried to soak up all the knowledge she could, paying close attention to detail. After gaining a little confidence in her own abilities, she would create her own looks and post them to her Instagram, which is where I found Debra's work.

Her makeup obsession started at a young age, but ironically, she couldn't start wearing makeup until the age of fifteen. Debra said, "I love creating makeup looks and have been obsessed with makeup and learning new makeup techniques since I was a young girl. My parents didn't allow me to wear makeup until I was fifteen. It was initially sixteen, but I begged and begged my mom to let me wear makeup all the time and she eventually gave in and lowered the age to fifteen. So, before I was allowed to actually wear makeup, I would take makeup quizzes to learn about products and read as much as I could about different makeup techniques and how applying makeup in different ways could accentuate different features and draw the eyes in different ways. This was in a time before YouTube existed, so my main sources of information were makeup company websites and various magazines." She was using her time wisely by studying makeup before she was even applying it.

Maintaining a full-time job and finding time to create and edit videos can be challenging, but Debra does it because she loves it so much. Because she dedicates all this time and effort to her videos, she hopes to keep growing her channel and one day start her own beauty line. Like I mentioned earlier, having a magnetic personality is essential to gaining loyal followers on YouTube. Luckily, Debra has the right personality to keep followers engaged. She said, "I like to be silly and don't think makeup should be boring, stuffy, or too rule-driven. People shouldn't be afraid of making mistakes when doing makeup, because makeup is art and should be fun, so I try to convey that in my videos and have as much fun as possible. I want my audience to have a fun time while learning new makeup tips and tricks!" Being too serious and rule-driven will only drive followers away. When people are watching YouTube videos to learn something, they want to connect with the person in the video and not be intimidated by what they are doing. Because people are tuning in to watch Debra Jenn's life through Instagram and YouTube, more makeup brands will want to put her on their PR lists to review and advertise their makeup. So far Debra has been doing ColourPop Cosmetics giveaways to her loyal followers.

Debra Jenn can teach us to not take ourselves too seriously. Let loose and show your personality to the camera. If you want to be a beauty resource for people like Debra is, start a YouTube account and dedicate social media pages to get your name noticed by others. Makeup companies reach out to people like Debra to promote their brands, giving you perks of free makeup and possible paid partnerships.

CHAPTER 25:

ANGELICA WHITE— MAKEUP BY ANGELICA

———

Being a self-starter in the makeup industry does not necessarily have to mean you are going out and generating a physical product. You can see this with the other great makeupreneurs I am featuring like Debra Jenn and Anjali Wrenn. It can simply mean that you are making a name for yourself in the beauty industry and/or providing beauty services.

While scrolling through Instagram, I came across a page called Makeup by Angelica. Her Instagram handle is @ makeupbyangelicaw. According to her Instagram bio, she is a self-taught makeup artist. I admire that she became great at makeup on her own, as not everybody who wants to be a makeupreneur wants to go to cosmetology school. It's always a learning experience with trial and error to get better.

Angelica White may be self-taught, but by scrolling through her Instagram page, it is quite evident that she has a natural talent for makeup artistry. Her looks incorporate bold eye makeup with a silky, luminous finish on the face. She is not afraid to dabble in unique eyeshadow color blends, and she sure isn't afraid to share her talent with the public, frequently showing off new looks to her more than two thousand followers. My favorite thing she does is step-by-step tutorials on her Instagram stories. They are engaging and informative for viewers who want to improve their makeup skills, me included. Her makeup looks can give you inspiration on how you want to wear your makeup on your wedding day, homecoming, birthday, or whatever the special occasion may be.

I wanted to know what was behind Angelica's beauty content and why she did it, so that's what I sought to find out. When I talked to Angelica, she told me she has always craved some sort of creative outlet. For a long time, she expressed herself through interior design and became quite good at it. "I grew up with a very handy father, so I wouldn't shy away from even the hardest projects. I have every tool under the sun in my garage and the list of the things I've built is pretty long," Angelica said. But life got in the way of her creative outlet of interior design, and her career in pharmaceutical marketing took over.

A true artist at heart, Angelica started to feel urges to create again after a long hiatus. That's when she turned to makeup videos on YouTube. She immersed herself in the world of makeup. Angelica's love for makeup grew immensely, partly because of Jaclyn Hill's YouTube videos. Jaclyn Hill is a very well-known YouTube personality who does makeup tutorials for a very wide, global audience. Her success has grown so large she even has collaborated with beauty brands BECCA Cosmetics and Morphe. Jaclyn Hill's YouTube channel is where I watched one of my first makeup tutorials ever, so I can understand the influence of makeup tutorials and Jaclyn Hill. It wasn't long before Angelica started to share her newfound passion for makeup online, primarily through Instagram.

Angelica's makeup has even been noticed by one of the biggest names in the makeup industry, Mario Dedivanovic, who is best known for being Kim Kardashian's makeup artist. Mario posted one of Angelica's makeup creations on his Instagram page, which is especially thrilling for someone like Angelica, who is self-taught and does it for the pure reason of expressing herself.

Ultimately, Angelica shares her work with others because she truly loves to. When I asked her why she wears makeup, she said, "I just feel like an upgraded version of myself. I love how you can enhance any look with a little makeup. I am a fairly confident person with or without makeup, but I just feel beautiful when my makeup is done." Personally, I strongly relate to this. Once you get skilled at makeup, it's hard to stop. There's a certain satisfaction you get once you are all dolled up and your makeup turned out well. This also reminds me of Huda Kattan, who used makeup for the excitement of enhancing one's appearance. It may seem trivial, but little excitements and passions like this is what motivates a successful makeupreneur.

As Angelica continues on with her journey, her goals are to get on PR lists for top brands; therefore, she can always have the latest and greatest beauty products to review for her followers. Some of her beauty staples include good skin care, the Anastasia Beverly Hills Brow Wiz, and the Tarte Shape Tape concealer. She brought up the point that skin care is more important than makeup itself. She said, "If your skin isn't right, your makeup will never look good." Your skin is the canvas, and you're going to want to have a healthy blank space to work on. A true makeupreneur cares about their skin care routine just as much as their makeup routine.

As far as anyone making it in the makeup industry, Angelica thinks it's possible. She said, "The makeup industry is really about expression of one's creativity. There will never be a lack of talent in the world, so if you have the will, then you can do it. It takes time and patience. As long as you couple that with content that people want to see you can succeed. The sky is the limit!" I adore Angelica's positivity. You can tell how much fun she has creating content for her viewers on Instagram. Angelica shows us that if you really love experimenting with makeup and sharing it with others, people and brands will catch on and want to follow your journey. Just by expressing yourself through makeup can turn you into a makeupreneur overnight.

CHAPTER 26:

CATHERINE ERWIN—LUNATICK COSMETIC LABS

———

Is Halloween your favorite time of the year? Are horror movies your favorite genre of movie? Do you like all things spooky and creepy? If you said yes to all of those things, then this makeup line is catered to you. I came across a company on Instagram called LunatiCK Cosmetic Labs, and I couldn't be happier. This is one of the coolest makeup brands I have ever encountered, and I am tempted to make a quick purchase. If you're into the dark, spooky aesthetic, then LunatiCK is a perfect makeup brand to explore. First of all, the packaging is spectacular. Eyeshadows are packaged in coffins with bat mirrors. Some of the names of the palettes include Vampira, Zombie Defense, Supernatural, and Elvira, Mistress Of The Dark. You can also buy individual shades as well, like Lime Lagoon and Myth. LunatiCK lipsticks really caught my eye as the tube is in shape of a gold bullet cartridge shape. In addition, they even have pressed powder in packaging in the shape of a Ouija board planchette, which I know a lot of people would get a kick out of. Why create a makeup line just like the rest? Creating fun makeup themes are a way to set yourself apart from the competition.

Before the creation of the LunatiCK, CEO Catherine Erwin started off working as a cosmetologist. Erwin said, "Art and beauty go hand in hand, and even before being licensed in cosmetology all aspect of art ruled my life, including photography, painting, and sculpting. Combining the two worlds happened organically with time." You can look at makeup as the paint and a makeup brush as the paintbrush. You can use different techniques that allow you to sculpt and highlight someone's face in the way you want. It truly is a form of art. Photography is often used to capture makeup on magazine covers and editorials and even to show beauty gurus displaying their work. This is not the case for everyone, but makeup is oftentimes a tool to express creativity. With LunatiCK, you can see the artwork and creativity shining through the makeup and the eye-catching packaging.

Working in the makeup industry may be an expression of art, but just like it's not easy to make it as an artist, it's not easy to make it in the makeup industry. LunatiCK's journey started in 2012 with Catherine Erwin handcrafting formulas made at home before handmade products were normalized. Catherine Erwin and her team worked for years to create the best makeup blends they could. Later, they were able to establish a headquarters in a chapel, where they had their own lab. As a self-starter, you can't expect every story to start out glamorously. Working in a lab, even though it was just a church, was an accomplishment. Two warehouse moves later, Catherine and her team are now in a 1,500-square-foot compound where they have a fully functioning in-house photography studio, marketing team, and fulfillment center. Catherine describes the industry as being cutthroat. The battle between being a good businesswoman and being an ethical businesswoman is constant. LunatiCK has chosen ethics. "There are many learning curves when you get involved in a billion-dollar industry, but as long as you stay true to yourself, you cannot lose," said Erwin. An ethical and eco-friendly company that genuinely has a great product is a win-win. As a consumer, you should do research before you buy. Makeup is expensive, so it's worth taking the extra time to look up a review, watch a YouTube tutorial, or read the ingredients in the product.

LunatiCK truly values high-quality products and customer satisfaction. Premium formulas are handcrafted by industry professionals and then sent to a leading chemist in the cosmetic industry for final assessment, tweaks, and testing to ensure a top-of-the-line product for beauty professionals and every day enthusiasts.

To be quite frank, Catherine knows not everyone can be a makeupreneur, even though she would love to say, "Yes, everyone can succeed in the beauty industry." It's cutthroat. She's seen good companies rise and fall simply from manipulation of the media. Competitors creating fake accounts to write bad reviews on your products is a real thing. It's impossible to be an entrepreneur in the industry without thick skin. Being in the limelight through any form of social media is putting you at risk of judgement and opposition.

Catherine Erwin's story shows us that you can release your creativity into makeup and make a bold statement as she did with LunatiCK's spunky style. It took her years to get where she is, not always taking the easy route. She gives us a heads-up that to survive in the industry, you need to be patient and be ready to deal with negative experiences.

Check out https://www.lunaticklabs.com/ to see Catherine's edgy makeup line.

CHAPTER 27:

JOYCE PLATON— HELLO BEAUTY

—

Podcasts are more popular than ever today. People are listening to them to stay awake on their way to work in the mornings or just listening to them throughout the day because a lot of good content is out there. It's a form of entertainment, but also a medium through which to learn something new. Podcasts have endless options to choose from, but in researching self-starters in the beauty industry, I came across Joyce Platon's podcast, "Hello Beauty."

Joyce Platon certainly has a unique and exciting role as a beauty influencer. It all started with a little chance. Her first career after college was a high-end corporate job. Being in such a professional position, Joyce wanted to look the part. This meant having the right clothes and wearing polished makeup. Joyce promptly enrolled herself in a high-end makeup class by the company Make Up For Ever. Going with a classy company like Make Up For Ever, Joyce was definitely in good hands. Makeup can be addicting, I know that, and Joyce became addicted to doing her makeup after her first class. She kept enrolling in more classes because it was a fun experience for her. She would then get invited to do makeup for fashion shows because her expertise was growing.

Next, she was asked to do magazine editorial work. Clearly those makeup classes payed off and created some awesome opportunities. Gradually, Joyce began to take on more makeup work and eventually became a part of the Make Up For Ever team because they saw potential in her. The fashion shows that Joyce worked for were all Make Up For Ever shows, such as Philippine Fashion Weeks and Metro Society Fashion Shows. When it comes to working for magazines, all were through Make Up For Ever and Shu Uemura. She also had multiple projects with *Preview Magazine, Candy Magazine, Esquire Magazine, For Him Magazine, Metro Society Magazine, METRO Magazine,* and *Rogue Magazine.* She even had direct bookings with *Rogue Magazine, Haute Punch Magazine, C-Heads Magazine, Preview Magazine, STATUS Magazine,* and *Reflex Homme.* Just by taking makeup classes to improve her professional appearance, opportunities arose that she never expected. Joyce didn't hesitate to take a leap of faith with Make Up For Ever.

On her website, Joyce Platon shares the editorial work and photoshoots she has worked on. I came across a magazine cover she did with Sofia Richie, who is an American model and the daughter of the iconic music artist, Lionel Richie. Joyce's makeup work is aesthetically pleasing, which attracts A-list celebrities and models to work with her. She stresses enhancing natural beauty, which I believe is the core idea of makeup.

Becoming a makeup artist happened by chance for Joyce, but she always had a fascination with beauty. She recalls growing up in the Philippines watching her mom get her hair and makeup done at salons. She even briefly cut hair and ran her own salon in the Philippines.

After ten years of working as a makeup artist in Los Angeles, she started to branch out and delve into beauty creative marketing and beauty podcasting. Her podcast is called "Hello Beauty." Joyce shared, "Its philosophy is to spread the word about discovering one's true inner beauty. I interview beauty industry experts and founders/CEOs of makeup and skin care brands and share their insights about the importance of inner beauty. The conversations are valuable because I get to share the message straight from the tastemakers and industry experts themselves." On her website you can see the exciting new people Joyce gets to talk to, one being Dr. Murad, who has one of the most well-known skin care lines in the United States and abroad called Murad. Joyce proves that to be a makeupreneur in the beauty industry doesn't necessarily mean you are creating new makeup products. She has given new meaning to being a self-starter in the beauty industry with her podcast. People are listening to her while on their way to work, relaxing at home, or at the gym. I think Joyce may be on to something big.

Joyce shows us that something as simple as having a conversation about beauty products can be a way of starting your entrepreneurial journey. In addition, something as simple as taking a makeup course to spruce up your makeup skills can have a lasting impact on your career. It's all about the simple measures you take that may lead you down a path of success.

Find this podcast at https://podcasts.apple.com/us/podcast/hello-beauty/id1434159680.

CONCLUSION

You may be the next makeupreneur, and that can mean whatever you want it to. Every makeupreneur I got to know does what they do because they truly love it. Some are more successful than others, but every one of them is fulfilling their passion. From local beauty salons to chemistry labs and even to the comfort of your own home, there may be something in this book that got you thinking "maybe I can do this, too."

If you see a disparity in the makeup industry, maybe you will be like Jackie Aina advocating for diversity in the beauty industry. If you are starting from ground zero, maybe you will be like Huda Kattan, who started by taking makeup classes and blogging every day until someone noticed her. You may be tech savvy and want to launch a beauty inspired app like Brandefy. You may have chronic acne and the only way to wear makeup that doesn't irritate your skin is by creating your own unique formula. Think about Shilpi Jain, CEO of Skinveda, and Chantal De Greef, CEO of Basic Beauty Tools, who created their lines based off of skin issues. Shilpi created her line for her son's eczema issues and Chantal did it because of her rare skin disease. You may be an artist at heart, and the best way to present that to others is to create a makeup line with eye-catching colors and a spunky design just like Wende Zomnir, creator of Urban Decay, and Catherine Erwin, creator of LunatiCK Cosmetic Labs. You may have a cause you want to support through makeup sales like Vanessa Amaya for childhood cancer awareness and Kayley and Blake Miller for animal shelters. You may be concerned with the chemicals in our beauty products like Gregg Renfrew, CEO of Beautycounter, or concerned with animals being harmed in the process of testing makeup, like Laura Cronin, the CEO of Clean-Faced Cosmetics.

Hearing everyone's story gets my mind racing about all of the possibilities of makeup. I think about the rush I felt wearing makeup as a dancer and all of the times I thought about having a makeup line of my own. Have an idea? Write it down. Keep it secret until you're ready to run with it. Collaborate with your closest friends and family to see if they can help you. Save up money so one day you can create a tangible product for the beauty community to gush over. In the meantime, use social media to build up your image, which costs zero dollars! If makeup is your passion, share that passion with others. You never know where it can lead you. All makeupreneurs may not be billionaires or megastars like Kylie Jenner or Rihanna, but they are making a living off of something that makes them happy, and you can, too.

APPENDIX

___

INTRODUCTION

Robehmed, Natalie. 2019. "At 21, Kylie Jenner Becomes the Youngest Self-Made Billionaire Ever." *Forbes.Com*. https://www.forbes.com/sites/natalierobehmed/2019/03/05/at-21-kylie-jenner-becomes-the-youngest-self-made-billionaire-ever/#6df264ce2794.

Panych, Sophia. 2019. "We Tried This Universal Highlighter on Every Skin Tone."

"Topic: Cosmetics Industry In The U.S.". 2019. *Www.Statista.Com*. https://www.statista.com/topics/1008/cosmetics-industry/.

CHAPTER 1

Huda Kattan." 2019. *Forbes*. https://www.forbes.com/profile/huda-kattan/#1215d68c3cec.

Kattan, Huda. "My makeup business story!" YouTube. http://www.youtube.com/watch?v=Vk41RBKVeho (May 05, 2019).

CHAPTER 2

"First-Ever Eyelash and Brow Artist-Industry Survey by Glad Lash Inc. Showcases a Highly Trained and Satisfied Group of Professionals." 2019. *Prnewswire.Com.* https://www.prnewswire.com/news-releases/first-ever-eye-lash-and-brow-artist-industry-survey-by-glad-lash-inc-showcases-a-highly-trained-and-satisfied-group-of-professionals-300488842.html.

"Why Is Microblading Going To Dominate The Beauty Industry in Years to Come?—*Phibrows USA—Art Of Beauty Academy.* https://www.artofbeautyacademy.com/microblading-dominates-beauty-industry/.

CHAPTER 5

Chang, Ciera, 2019. "As Told By: Lavonndra Elle Johnson-Digital Beauty." *Digital Beauty.* https://digitalbeauty.com/lavonndra-elle-johnson/.

CHAPTER 9

Eldor, Karin. 2018. "How Laura Mercier Has Remained a Force in Beauty, After More Than 20 Years." *Forbes.Com.* https://www.forbes.com/sites/karineldor/2018/09/30/how-laura-mercier-has-remained-a-force-in-beauty-more-than-20-years-later/#676da23258fa.

"Laura Mercier Competitors, Revenue, Number of Employees, Funding and Acquisitions." 2019. *Owler*. https://www.owler. com/company/lauramercier.

CHAPTER 10

Brown, Bobbi. 2007. "How I Did it: Bobbi Brown, Founder and CEO, Bobbi Brown Cosmetics." *Inc.*, 2007. https://www.inc. com/magazine/20071101/how-i-did-it-bobbi-brown-founder-and-ceo-bobbi-brown.html.

CHAPTER 11

ABC. 2017. "#3 Wende Zomnir, Urban Decay." Podcast. No Limits With Rebecca Jarvis.

"About CEW—Cosmetic Executive Women." 2019. Cosmetic Executive Women. https://www.cew.org/about-cew/.

CHAPTER 12

Gharib, Susie. 2019. "Ulta CEO Says of Her Success: 'Anything Is Possible' With Hard Work." Fortune. https://fortune. com/2019/01/15/ulta-beauty-ceo-mary-dillon-leadership/.

CHAPTER 13

Houlis, Annamarie. 2018. "How Jackie Aina Went From Army Reservist to Beauty Influencer Phenomenon and Activist." Fashionista. https://fashionista.com/2018/06/jackie-aina-makeup-youtube.

"NAACP | About-Us." 2019. NAACP. https://www.naacp.org/.

CHAPTER 14

ABC. 2017. "#23: Gregg Renfrew, Beautycounter Founder and CEO." Podcast. No Limits With Rebecca Jarvis.

CHAPTER 15

Cheng, Andrea. 2019. "Why You Should Care About Vegan Beauty." Nytimes.Com. https://www.nytimes.com/2019/02/26/style/why-you-should-care-about-vegan-beauty.html.

CHAPTER 16

"Welcome to African Herstory-Black Girl Magic Lives and Rules Here." 2019. Welcome to African Herstory. https://www.africanherstory.com/.

"WARIF—Women at Risk International Foundation." 2019. Warifng.Org. https://warifng.org/.

Made in the USA
San Bernardino, CA
26 February 2020